LATIN TODAY

HODIE LATINA

To Patrick and Diana with best wishes!

7 : viii : 2013

John Gray

LATIN TODAY
HODIE LATINA

John Gray

Published by Canis Press
Little Hollies
Bonnington, Kent
TN25 7 AZ

First published in Great Britain 2007
© John Gray 2007-08-20

ISBN 978-0-9548878-1-0

Design, typesetting and production by
John Saunders Design & Production, Abingdon OX13 5HU
Printed in Great Brtain by Biddles Ltd., King's Lynn

FOREWORD

Latin Today and Every Day

When, many years ago, I left school and with it all those years of toil over a Latin Primer and more complicated texts, I thought never to see the language or to need it again. I could not have been more wrong.

It is everywhere around us. Regimental mottoes, squadron emblems, service insignia are steeped in it. We see it on inscriptions, statues, monuments and epitaphs. Old churches, abbeys, cloisters and academic colleges cannot do without it Even in AD 2007 it is inscribed anew on the £5 Crown struck by the Royal Mint to mark HM the Queen's diamond wedding anniversary. Latin assails us in one form or another every day, and not just in the ecclesiastic, academic or judicial professions. No country which has ever gone through the Roman occupation, the Dark Ages, Renaissance and Enlightenment will ever be free of it.

Even the society that once used it as a daily Lingo is with us at every turn. Rome is never out of the cinema or library, never off the TV screen. Rome dominated the known world longer than any other conqueror or empire, including ours, and wherever the legions paused someone produced a hammer and chisel and began to chip away on a nearby rock. The legion's equivalent of Kilroy appears to have got everywhere.

So 2000 years later even one with no erudition (I hint of course at this writer) can appear to have the semblance of learning by translating what Kilroy chipped to an admiring audience of fellow tourists.

But one needs help, specifically John Gray's help. Some years ago he produced 'Lawyers' Latin' which explained (comprehensibly, sometimes amusingly) those hundreds of phrases with which the Legal profession seeks, pretty successfully and expensively, to baffle the rest of us. Then came 'Long Live Latin', a simple alphabetical list of Latin words and phrases with translation and accompanying commentary, informative and intermittently entertaining.

Now appears 'Latin Today', broken down into headings such as 'mottos' and 'coinage' etc., and with fulsome explanations over and above simple translations Here is not simply the 'what does it mean?' of the Latin tag, but also ' where does it come from, who first said it, in what circumstances?'

In a new departure the author gives us pen portraits of some of the more notable or infamous Roman Emperors, and even invades the realm of medieval academia to provide translation of the dog Latin of the Bayeux Tapestry.

A slim book for the Christmas stocking and very useful also to slip into the luggage before any touristic venture and thus amaze fellow tourists with a wholly meretricious pretence of having a classical education.

Frederick Forsyth
Hertford September 2007

TO ALL OUR ANIMALS

Bertie and Ivo
(dogs)

Apollo and Poppy
(ponies)

Cleopatra, Larry
Florian and Aida
(sheep)

CONTENTS

J'y perd mon Latin

'I Can't make head or tail of it' or 'I'm at my wit's end' or 'It's beyond me' or 'I give up' or I can't make sense of it'. French idiomatic expression and some English possible equivalents.

What would we do today without some knowledge of Latin?

ACKNOWLEDGEMENTS

My thanks and gratitude to:

My wife, Susie, for drawings and calligraphy introducing the illustrations to each caption heading and for producing them even better than I could have hoped for.

The Royal Mint for permission to reproduce the inscription TUEATUR UNITA DEUS in the design context (of Emma Noble) in which it appears on the £5 crown struck in 2007 to mark the Diamond Wedding Anniversary of HM Queen Elizabeth II. This coin initiated and was the *sine qua non* of producton of this book. The design of this coin is the subject of Crown Copyright.

John Weeks QC, sometime classical scholar of Worcester College, Oxford, and *quondam* Judge Weeks, for endlessly helping me out with translation and generally.

Dr. Roger Tomlin, of Wolfson College, Oxford, for being so generously approachable and, with his great knowledge and expertise, affording the kind of guidance and assistance for which I could scarcely have hoped.

John Parker for some helpful proof reading and for very kindly permitting me to reproduce extracts from his book *Reading Latin Epitaphs. A Handbook for Beginners*.

Tom Kemp for once again providing his supreme lettering and design talent and skills in producing for me another jacket.

Camilla Smallwood for valuable guidance and authoritative advice giving insight into the world of publishing.

Anna Gray for putting my laptop computer to greater use than my own very limited technological skills permitted: in particular in working wonders with indexing. For doing too a lot of typing which at my own veteran speeds would have taken me an eternity.

Theresa Kirkpatrick (Née Gray) for looking up numerous facts which I was too computer-phobic to find for myself.

Eight word extract from James Hilton's 'Goodbye Mr. Chips' (Copyright © James Hilton 1934) reproduced by permission of Hodder and Stoughton Limited.

B.J. Lenon Esq, M.A., Head Master of Harrow School, for kind permission to reproduce the fourth verse of a School song entitled *Stet Fortuna Domus*.

Brian Sewell for permission to quote from and use his article 'Why I shall continue to feed the Pigeons' published in The Evening Standard on the nineteenth January 2007.

Amministrazione del Patrimonio della Sede Apostolica (Administration of the Patrimony of the Apostolic See, Vatican City) for permission to reproduce and quote words of Pope John XXIII.

PREFACE

Why Latin in 2007? Well because it is far from a dead language. Practically nobody can speak it, an elite few can read it with varying degrees of comprehension, while the great majority have scant or no knowledge whatsoever. Yet, whether they like it or not, they will keep on coming across it and too many will have no remote idea of what it means or of what, if any, importance is to be attached to it today. They will miss much, for the message from the Latin words can be so rewarding, if understood!

How many know what means the inscription, *Tueatur Unita Deus* (see page 24 under 'AD 2007'), on the five pound 2007 silver crown struck by The Royal Mint to mark H.M. The Queen's Diamond Wedding? Inscribed on the reverse and in the surround to an attractive design following the pattern of the North Rose Window at Westminster Abbey, the words translate as 'may God guard these united'. In a year when the Scottish Nationalist Party vociferously urges Scottish independence, it is worth noting that this inscription was last used on coinage in 1603-4 by King James VIth of Scotland and Ist of England, reference being to his two newly united kingdoms.

In a year when Pope Benedict XVI has called for more Latin in the liturgy of the Roman Catholic Church, when a special 2007 coin is inscribed with Latin and when David Beckham has on him Latin tattoos, it may be time to take a little look at some of the language.

In this very short volume is set out under headings a selection of Latin words and phrases, which may be encountered and which, translated, may be found in varying degree rewarding, useful, interesting, informative, entertaining and in most instances, in one way or another, relevant to today. Some are simply words of wisdom, for that is a quality little changed and just as valuable today as it was hundreds of years ago. Nearly all have a nexus with some aspect of the year AD 2007, though this may sometimes be tenuous and not always obvious.

A political book was not intended but, on becoming Prime Minister, Gordon Brown drew attention to his old school motto. This was reproduced in its original Latin by some newspapers and promoted interest in mottos (many of them in Latin) and thereby prompted reference to other Latin material, which may have relevance to him and invite comment of a political nature.

In a book devoted to Romans and the Latin language, I have orientated the historical as much to Britain as possible. How many know that in the year AD 193 the Roman governor of the Province of Britannia, one Clodius Albinus, was declared Roman Emperor by the legions he commanded and that in AD 286 one Carausius, Roman commander of the British North Sea Fleet, declared himself emperor of Britain, quite independent of Rome?

On the acknowledgements page I have thanked a number of people in terms which I hope reflect my real heartfelt gratitude. I have been saved from too much error. I have not however always followed advice to the letter, so that any and all errors remaining are are almost certainly mine.

Those who have read Harry Mount's 'Amo, Amas, Amat . . ' will of course already have learnt, or heavily revised a forgotten knowledge of, the Latin language and may be sufficiently enthused to put this to good use, to read here a little more and to appreciate its relevance to today.

This is a Romano-British book: Latin for 2007. *Lege feliciter!* (read happily! The Venerable Bede).

JOHN GRAY
October 2007

A.D. 2007

Some Latin phrases and expressions have a real relevance in AD 2007. Here are a few:

Age dum, mora noxia, cras nil 'do it now. Delay is dangerous. There is no tomorrow'. The world is wakening up to global warming at last as the ice caps melt away, the polar bears drown and sea levels rise. Do something now! This inscription appears in glass on the upper floor of the Old Ashmolean in Oxford. *Dimidium facti qui coepit habet sapere aude* 'to have begun is half the battle: be sensible and bold'. Horace Ars Poetica 40. Just get going!

A fortiori 'with stronger (reason or force)'. An expression much used by lawyers as they advance an argument or reason carrying greater force than that which preceded it. An example of its use not law related, and all too relevant today, may assist understanding: 'those who are overweight ought not to eat chocolate biscuits; *a fortiori* they ought not to eat doughnuts! or sausages and chips'!

Alchymista spem alit aeternam 'scientific research keeps hope alive for ever.' Words written at the rear of the Dyson Perrin's Laboratory in Oxford. Will scientists find an answer to global warming and a means of disposing safely of nuclear waste? Will cures be found for progressive, particularly neurological, degenerative disease? *Dum spiro spero* 'while I breath I hope'.

> 'Hope, like the gleaming taper's light
> Adorns and cheers our way,
> And still as darker grows the night
> Emits a brighter ray'.
>
> Oliver Goldsmith 1728–1774.

Anno Domini 'in the year of our Lord'. Abbreviated to AD. The exact date of Christ's birth is unknown but the commencement date for western calendars is arbitrarily accepted. Dating in this way was introduced in the 6th century by a monk from one time Scythia (the Danube delta) called Dionysius Exiguus. The letters AD should be placed before the number whereas the letters BC (before Christ – English!) should be placed after. 'AD' as an expression is often used colloquially to denote old age: "My memory is failing, it must be a question of AD".

Brittunculi. Derogatory word for the British found at Vindolanda, a Roman fort and settlement just south of Hadrian's Wall. Referring to the unruly and bellicose tribes in the vicinity this word has been translated variously as 'the wretched or bloody Brits'. It is not classical Latin. In recent times this word might have been used for British lager louts abroad.

Ceteris paribus 'other things being equal'. As we board this 'Dicey Airways' flight for Rome, *ceteris paribus* we should be there in a few hours. *Deo volente* 'God willing' might be just as good an expression!

Internexus 'the internet'. Not classical Latin! Language update.

Nihil est ab omni parte beatum 'nothing is blessed from all sides'. Horace Odes II.xvi.27. Nothing is an unmixed blessing. No good thing is without a downside somewhere. Every bonus we get is taxed.

Nihil tam munitum quod non expugnare pecunia possit 'nothing is so well fortified that money cannot capture it'. Cicero In Verrem 1.ii.4. Few people can't be bought and no company, however big, is safe in 2007 from leveraged takeover. Alliance Boots, Sainsbury, ICI? The words are from a speech made by Cicero in 70BC successfully prosecuting G. Verres a more than usually corrupt Roman ex-governor of Sicily. The prosecution was successful despite bribery and engagement of the illustrious advocate Q. Hortensius to defend. Seneca observed: *'ab honesto virum nihil deterret* ' nothing deters a good man from honesty'. Yet the old English adage is 'every man has his price!!'

Nolite fumare 'do not smoke'. To smoke in so many places is an offence in both England and Scotland since the Health Act 2006 came into force in 2007 so that *interdictum est fumare* 'forbidden to smoke' might be better. NB (*nota bene*) for *ignorantia juris (legis) neminem excusat* 'ignorance of the law excuses nobody.' *Nolite fumare* is not a classical Latin expression because Romans didn't smoke. Remember too *flamma fumo est proxima* 'there's no smoke without fire'.

Nos numerus sumus et fruges consumere nati 'we are a category born to use up resources.' Horace 65-8 BC. Epistles i.ii.27. How true still in 2007 as we run out of fossil fuel and destroy the rain forests.

O tempora! O mores! 'what times, what customs.' Cicero In Catilinam i, 2. Things are not what they used to be. It seems they never were. From perhaps Cicero's most famous speech made against Catiline who, having failed to secure the means to bring about much needed economic reform, plotted violent seizure of the necessary power. The words are much quoted and might sometimes be loosely translated as 'good grief'. Conveys well our reaction to so much of what we read in the newspapers.

Pediludium 'football.' Not classical Latin!' Necessary update. Another is *birota*, 'bicycle', a word coined by a Cardinal writing Latin encyclicals.

Persona non grata 'unacceptable person or one who has incurred disfavour'. The guest who drinks too much and regularly spills red wine in your house will almost certainly become *persona non grata*. So too will the fellow whose ferocious snarling Doberman habitually threatens your gentle, elderly, much loved Labrador (the author has lurchers!). There are plenty of people around for whom this expression might be suitable, particularly among politicians and bureaucrats. The expression's origin however was in diplomatic circles where it referred to one who was unacceptable to a King or Government. *Persona grata* means the opposite.

Quod di omen avertant 'heaven forbid'. Goes for so much proposed by government.

Rubicon. Name of a river which ran between Cisalpine Gaul and Italy. In 49 BC the Roman senate directed Julius Caesar to disband his army in Gaul and warned that to cross this river without doing so would mean civil war. Caesar crossed with the words (according to Suetonius) *iacta est alea* 'the die is cast'. The expression 'to cross the Rubicon' has come to be used in the English language to describe the taking of a risky step from which there is no going back. Nobody now knows where geographically this famous river Rubicon was. Men and women 'cross the Rubicon' every day when they resign their jobs and embark upon the uncertainty of new ones.

Sic semper tyranis 'thus ever to tyrants'. Attributed to an outburst of John Wilkes Booth after he had shot and killed Abraham Lincoln in 1865. Useful words to direct to many tiresome bureaucrats, preferably after inflicting on them some comeuppance humiliation: short of death! Also the motto of the State of Virginia.

Sideralis navis 'spaceship'. Not classical Latin!. Update.

Stultior stulto fuisti, qui tabellis crederes 'you are stupider than stupid if you believe what is written'. Plautus (c. 250-184 BC) *Curculio*, 551. It is no guarantee of truth that something is written or in print. Don't necessarily believe what you read in newspapers. This seems to have been valuable advice from time immemorial.

Tempora (omnia) mutantur et nos mutamur in illis 'times (all things) change and we change with them'. Tony Blair has been succeeded by Gordon Brown. Things will change? For the better or for the worse? What odds are Ladbrokes giving? How soon will we know?

Tueatur Unita Deus 'may God guard those united'. Inscription on a five pound crown coin struck by The Royal Mint in 2007 for the Diamond Wedding anniversary of H.M.Queen Elizabeth II. The words are on the reverse in the surround, and an integral part of a pleasing design (by Emma Noble) following the pattern of the North Rose Window at Westminster Abbey. A Crown is traditionally a 25p (or five shilling) coin whereas this is five pounds. It is legal tender and struck in cupro-nickel.

The phrase has been inscribed before on English, Scottish and Irish coins of King James I. '*Those united*' whom God was to guard referred then to the recently united kingdoms of Scotland and England. With the endeavours and ambitions of the Scottish Nationalist Party these words might again in 2007 be invoked in this sense and context. The Royal Mint however confirmed the *status quo* in 2007 by striking a £2 coin commemorating the 300th centenary of the Act of Union 1707 with an edge inscription 'United into One Kingdom'. See under Coinage at page 96 below.

Una salus victis nullam sperare salutem 'the only safe course for the vanquished is to expect no mercy'. Virgil Aeneid ii 343. For this, and for reasons of honour, a defeated Roman fell on his sword. In April 2007 British and American forces occupied Iraq following the defeat and later execution of Saddam Hussein. At this time western relations with neighbouring Iran were at a low ebb owing to the belief that that country sought to develop nuclear weapons. British military personnel were captured and detained for allegedly trespassing in Iranian territorial waters. They were released after a period of very considerable concern for their safety. Iran, however, by this ostensible civilised clemency pulled off a much better public relations exercise than the UK government, which became quickly plunged into controversy by apparently seeking to retrieve ground lost by permitting those released to sell the story of their experiences to the media and then (once the deed was done by two of them) withdrawing the authorisation which had contravened acknowledged service practice and caused outrage in the nation and particularly in senior army and naval circles.

Concern for those detained might well have been well founded and the modern equivalent of falling on a sword might have been realistically contemplated by them. The Persians have in the past shown a cruel and devious streak. As long ago as AD 260 the beleaguered Roman Emperor, Valerian, faced the advance of an aggressive Persia led by one Shapur, who sought to regain provinces lost to the Romans. The defending Roman army was beset by plague. The Emperor sought to extricate his forces by negotiation and at the demand of Shapur attended personally upon him, accompanied by only a small retinue of high-ranking officials. All were seized and captured. Valerian is said to have been humiliated for some years (he was forced to act as a human foot-stool for Shapur to mount his horse) before being tortured and put to death and his stuffed body publicly displayed *in terrorem*. Valerian had been a fierce persecutor of Christians who, doubtless, saw his fate as a due and righteous comeuppance.

Ultimus Romanorum 'the last of the Romans'. Brutus's tribute to the dead Cassius who in 44BC had been a fellow assassin of Julius Caesar. Words attributed by Plutarch. Brutus 84. The murderous actions of Brutus and Cassius and others were seen in many quarters as worthy, directed to preserving the Roman Republic from the grasp of an imminent emperor already dictator. The expression appears in Shakespeare's Julius Caesar

(V.iii.99). 'The last of all the Romans fare thee well!'. We may have seen the last of the Romans but we have not seen the last of their language. *Vivat Lingua Latina*! 'long live the Latin language'.

HOLIDAY/TOURISM

Plaques, statues, buildings and other objects bearing Latin inscriptions or Latin names are more likely to be encountered and to arouse curiosity when sightseeing, on holiday or touring. A little enlightening background information is usually acceptable. See too under Epitaphs and Bayeux Tapestry at pages 48 and 111 respectively below.

Bonum vinum laetificat cor hominis 'good wine cheers the heart of man'. Popular French adage to be seen in France on walls of restaurants. It is based on Psalm 104:15. 'And wine that maketh glad the heart of man'. With such welcome effect and authoritative sanction, who would be teetotal?

Classicianus. Name of the procurator (financial administrator) for the Roman Province of Britannia (Britain) AD 61-65. Take a London Underground train (District or Circle line) to Tower Hill. Leave the station and then turn right down stone steps at the foot of which, on the left, will be found a bronze statue of a Roman, thought to be of the Emperor Trajan. Set in the wall nearby is a plaque commemorating one Gaius Julius Alpinus Classicianus. Who was this man? Why commemorate so elaborately a Roman Procurator? Thought to have been a Gaul, he was, for the times a man of great humanity. Though he does not get a good press from Tacitus, it appears that he used his utmost endeavours to restore peace and civilisation in the province of Britannia after the defeat of Boadicea's (Boudicca's) rebellion, following which pockets of still belligerent Britons were hunted down and treated to the utmost brutality by the military victor and governor, Suetonius Paulinus. Classicianus finds mention in book 14 of Tacitus' '*Annale*s . . . . *Ab excessu divi Augusti* ' 'Annals from the death of the divine emperor Augustus' (available in Penguin Classics' translation as 'Tacitus. The Annals of Imperial Rome') and parts of his tombstone, erected by his 'sorrowing wife, Julia Pacata', are in the British Museum. The plaque was put up following their discovery in 1852 and 1935. See Boadicea under Historical at page 99 below.

Cloaca maxima 'the main drain (of Rome)'. Famous part of Rome's drainage and sewage system. Built circa 100 BC it drains into the River Tiber and remains today a part of the drainage system.

Colosseum. Name of the great 'Flavian Amphitheatre' in Rome. Illustrated above, it was substantially built by the emperor Vespasian and completed by his son Titus in AD 80. Its completion was followed by celebration in the form of one hundred days of appalling bloody gladiatorial and wild beast contests witnessed by countless citizens of the western world's then most civilised nation. It was capable of holding more than 50,000 spectators and could be flooded so as to make possible mock sea battles. Still standing today, it is very impressive.

Columbus 'pigeon or dove'. The pigeons in Trafalgar Square have for many years been one of London's great attractions.

Fearless and friendly they provided the greatest of fun for children and adult alike: to feed, to watch and to see the wild close up. But they are threatened with a final solution in the form of a mass death warrant, a decree of 'columbal extermination' (from the Gauleiter of London, Ken Livingstone). The word 'cull' seems to mean licence for the mass murder by man for his own ends of other defenceless living things; sheep and cattle (foot and mouth disease), birds (avian flu) and badgers (tuberculosis). This however is not even a cull. There is nothing selective about it. A complete eradication is intended. In ranting language Livingstone asserts that pigeons are the vermin of the air, flying rats as filthy as those beneath our feet in London's sewers, contagious communicators of disease and plague, *Columbus bubonicus*. The Westminster council has applied for a new by-law banning pigeons from what is their last remaining sanctuary, the north terrace outside the National Gallery.

In the Evening Standard of 19:1:07 writer and art critic Brian Sewell wrote a Ciceronian *pro columbo* ('for or on behalf of the pigeon') and/or an 'against Livingstone'. The pigeon is the avian equivalent not of the rat but of man's best friend, the dog. He eulogises on the pigeon's honoured place in antiquity. This bird is one for whom over the centuries we have built dovecotes in our houses, who is adored and pampered by the fraternity who know him and for which he races. Born and bred in London, Mr. Sewell has in 75 years been shat upon by a pigeon only once and then quickly realised the good fortune said to follow such a happening; he found a £20 note with no conceivable owner in sight. London is not decimated by plague. All together then, Londoners, Latinists and tourists: "long live the pigeons, *vivant columbi, vivan las palomas, vivent les pigeons, es leben die Tauben . . . . À bas* (down with) *lapis vivens* 'Livingstone'.

Dominus custodiat introitum tuum et exitum tuum 'may the Lord preserve thy going in and thy going out'. From the Vulgate Psalm 121.8. Most tourists and holidaymakers will go to Oxford and will probably visit the historic University Church of St. Mary the Virgin in Radcliffe Square. On their way out, cut into the side facing the church of one of the stone steps, which they mount, they will see the above Latin words. Strategically placed with laudable skill they are seen only when the visitor has been in and is going out.

Durotriges. See under Historical at page 101 below.

Hadrianus. Emperor Hadrian (Publius Aelius Hadrianus) AD 117–138. An energetic and efficient ruler who visited nearly the whole of the Roman Empire. He was a great builder. His sumptuous Villa near Tivoli at the foot of the Sabine Hills is a must for every tourist. For the British holidaymaker or foreign tourist in Britain of particular interest is the wall he caused to be built as part of a great plan to strengthen the frontiers of the Roman Empire and, in this instance, particularly to separate Romans from barbarians.

Stretching some 73 miles across northern England from Tyne to Solway, it is a remarkable and vast feat of construction with turrets every Roman mile (a Roman mile was a thousand double paces, about 1611 English yards). Commenced in AD122, when Hadrian visited Britain, it took only about ten years to complete. Much of it survives and a good starting point is Vindolanda near Hexham in Northumberland, where archaeological excavation is ongoing and all manner of fascinating finds are on view in the nearby Chesterholm Museum, Bardon Mill.

Hadrian's visit to Britain was marked by the minting of a *sestertius* coin commemorating the occasion and showing the emperor's head: on the reverse appears almost the earliest personalised Britannia sitting very much as she has been seen on British coinage since the reign of Charles II and currently on the reverse of 50p pieces. On some uncirculated coins she has been portrayed in her chariot. Shame on Gordon Brown's suggestion in 2006, that she should be removed and replaced by something more suitable to 'Cool Britannia'. Fortunately the Royal Mint has responded by striking in 2007 a set of six £1 silver Proof Britannia Coins and a series of Britannia gold coins with a newly designed Britannia shown on their reverse, seated with trident, Union Jack oval shield, olive branch and, lying at her feet guarding, a formidably large British Lion, suitably cross, fierce and forbidding looking. Design is by Christopher Le Brun. R.A.

Quocunque jeceris stabit 'whichever way you throw it, it will stand up'. If you visit the Isle of Man, there is every chance that you will come across its coat of arms incorporating a three legged emblem (each leg usually clad in armour) and the above Latin words. It is nice to know what thy mean. Found on a sword and on a stone cross, this was adopted in the 12th century as the island's symbol.

Re(g)ina liberta coniunx. See under Slavery at page 82 below.

Scottorum malleus 'hammer of the Scots'. Remarkable as an epitaph. Those visiting Westminster Abbey will find, if they look carefully, these words inscribed on the Purbeck (a freshwater limestone quarried on the isle of Purbeck in Dorset) marble tomb of King Edward I. The full epitaph reads *Edwardus primus Scottorum malleus hic est 1308 pactum serva* 'here lies Edward I, the hammer of the Scots. Keep troth (faith or loyalty)'.

As a renowned jurist King Edward arbitrated in 1292 on the

disputed Scottish succession and pronounced in favour of John Balliol. The latter's nobles influenced him into alliance with France in order to mitigate English influence. Already warring in France, Edward was enraged and summoned Balliol to meet him at Berwick. On advice Balliol declined. Berwick was sacked with a ferocity which shocked, even in those hardy, long-suffering times. Balliol surrendered his crown and Scotland came under English administration.

Then emerged a stalwart leader of men and a champion of Scottish Nationalism possessed of remarkable natural military flair: the redoubtable William Wallace. At Stirling he smashed the army of the English northern administration. Edward negotiated peace with France, then turned the full might of feudal England against Wallace and at the battle of Falkirk inflicted devastating defeat on the Scots. See it all (not entirely historically accurately) in the film Braveheart.

In 1296 on return from his Scottish campaign, King Edward brought to England from Scone the stone of destiny, which had been integral in the crowning of the Kings of Scotland. He had a chair made to hold it (in a space beneath the seat). This has been used at every coronation since 1308 and may be seen in Westminster Abbey (without the stone). In a daring raid at Christmas 1950 the stone was removed from the Abbey by Scottish Nationalists and taken back to Scotland. It was recovered, but in 1996 was returned to Scotland where it now rests but will be lent and used in England on the occasion of future coronations.

Not far away outside Charing X Station is to be seen evidence of another side to this stern King's character. The capable *Scottorum malleus* was devastated by the death in 1290 of his beloved wife, Eleanor of Castile, at Harby, Nottinghamshire. A grieving cortège bore her body for burial in Westminster Abbey and on the long route stopped twelve times for rest. At each such place the distraught king ordered a stone cross to be built in her memory. 'The Eleanor Crosses'. There were twelve such crosses, only three of which survive at: Northampton, Geddington and Waltham Cross. That now at Charing X, the last stopping place before burial, is an eighteenth century reconstruction of a cross originally sited nearer to the Abbey. Nothing on the monument existing today tells its moving story, known to too few.

SPQR abbreviation of '*Senatus Populusque Romanus*' 'The senate (governing body of Rome) and the Roman People.' The letters appeared on standards which were carried at the head of Roman armies. In modern Rome they are to be seen on buses and on drain covers.

Tabula (in) naufragio See under General/Miscellaneous at page 47 below.

Trajan, Marcus Ulpius Trainus. Roman Emperor AD 98-117. A bronze statue thought to be of him is to be seen just outside Tower Hill underground station in London. He was a Spaniard and the first emperor not of Italian origin. His massive column in Rome depicts in stone pictorial relief his victories over the Dacians. At the foot of the column an inscription is written in capital lettering (*majusculae*) used today as the basis of our own capital lettering.

Vercingetorix. See under Historical at page 103 below.

POLITICAL

In a year of Prime Ministerial change it might be useful for politicians to know and sometimes to heed some of those Latin expressions below set out.

Ad captandum vulgus 'to attract or win over the crowd'. Appeal to the caprice of the mob. The objective of nearly every politician. The question is, does he or she behave like a shyster in exploiting it? For the avoidance of doubt the word 'shyster' is not vulgar abuse and means one who achieves his ends by means which are unscrupulous (which includes lying). It is a word used usually by lawyers and is directed frequently against other lawyers.

Dona clandestina semper sunt suspiciosa 'secret gifts are always suspicious.' Cash for honours? The Romans were well acquainted with corruption. *Beneficium accipere libertatem est vendere* 'to accept a favour is to sell one's liberty' wrote Publilius Syrus in the first century BC., a man who came to Rome as a slave, was manumitted (freed) and wrote a series of moral maxims for schools, *sententiae*, from which this is taken.

Dux femina facti 'the leader of the enterprise a woman'. Aeneid i 364 in which Venus tells Aeneas of Dido's courageous qualities. A piece of Virgil which appeals greatly to the feminists. Do we need another Margaret Thatcher?

Fide sed cui vide 'trust but watch (take care) in whom'. The new Prime Minister, Gordon Brown, immediately on assuming office urged the restoration of trust between government and the electorate. That must be an up-hill task (*adverso flumine* 'against the stream!) when the leader of the band himself has spent more than ten years imposing stealth taxes and too often has failed to mention them in his budget speeches, leaving them to emerge later from the small print. Sir Walter Raleigh, 1552-1618, warned his son (the two pictured together in a portrait to be seen in the Tudor Room at the National Portrait Gallery) 'trust no man too much'.

Gaudeamus igitur juvenes dum sumus 'let us rejoice while we are young'. These well known words are from a revised medievel drinking song.

'Time the subtle thief of youth' wrote John Milton 1608-1674. Ninety days detention without charge or trial, a real thief of time, liberty and justice. Nothing subtle about such state authorised theft.

See *satius est impunitum* below at page 38.

Nescis mi, fili, quantilla prudentia mundus regatur 'you do not know my son with what a small stock of wisdom the world is governed'. Attributed to Oxenstern (1583-1684) (chancellor to King Gustav Adolph II of Sweden) whose outstanding administrative and diplomatic qualities enabled him to negotiate favourable peace treaties with Denmark (1613), Russia (1617) and Poland (1629). He was a man in a position to talk. Are world leaders endowed with any more wisdom today? Might not *satis eloquentiae, sapientiae parum* 'plenty of eloquence (but) too little wisdom' still be the order of the day? See *vir sapit qui pauca loquitur* under Social below.

Non pudet vanitatis? 'are you not ashamed of your folly?' Use of Latin in the Treasury was abolished in 1995 and so the *quondam* (sometime) Chancellor of the Exchequer might not understand if this expression were to be put to him *inter alia* in relation to his de-stabilising of pension funds by abolition of the tax credit and to his disastrously ill-judged and unnecessary sale of UK gold reserves at a twenty year low price, losing the country millions. The nation may be forgiven for quoting Latin to him now that he has become Prime Minister: *speramus meliora* 'we hope for better things'.

Omnium consensu capax imperii nisi imperasset 'all were agreed that he was fit to rule if only he hadn't'. Said by Tacitus of the emperor Galba. Historiae 1,49. After the atrocities of Nero's reign and his unseemly death, Galba, a man of 70 years, was urged to 'rescue the human race'. He became Emperor in AD 68 and had his coinage inscribed with the words *salus humani generis* 'rescuer or salvation of the human race' and *libertas restituta, Roma renascens* 'liberty restored, Rome being reborn'. His reign lasted some eight months before he was brutally murdered by the praetorian guard, being unwilling to pay the price of their support. Plutarch tells us that his last words were "do your job if this is better for the Roman people". *Libertas restituta* will hardly have application in UK with the new Prime Minister's support for a 90 day period of detention without charge or trial for 'suspected' terrorists': see *satius est impunitum . . .* below.

Oratio congratulatoria 'congratulatory speech'. The kind of speech in self-congratulation the nation hears from Government Ministers whenever they can manage it without obvious ridicule.

Quomodo Adulator ab Amico Internoscatur 'how a flatterer is to be distinguished from a friend'. Latin title to a treatise written by the Greek historian and moral philosopher Plutarch. Essential reading for new Prime Ministers. In the end John Major felt himself constrained to complain about 'the bastards' in his party.

Reorganisation is a wonderful thing for creating the illusion of progress whilst producing confusion, inefficiency and demoralisation. This is set out in the English because it is so often thus quoted and attributed to Petronius Arbiter (died AD 65): but quoted without original Latin or reference to any work. They are words which certainly could have been said or written by a man of his wit, ability and spirit. The source and any original Latin however seem to be bogus and the authorship of Petronius is questioned. They could too be said to apply to the consequential effect of just about every cabinet re-shuffle and to the outcome of the recommendations made by so many public inquiries.

Petronius himself became a provincial governor, was writer of a long satirical work 'Satyricon' (deriding entertainingly the vulgarity of excessive riches . . .only a relatively small part of which survives) and was admitted to the emperor Nero's inner circle as *arbiter elegantiae* 'judge of elegance or of good taste', a description and a pun (said by Tacitus Annals xvi 18). Wrongly accused of plotting the Emperor's downfall, he was ordered to commit suicide. He cut his veins, then quickly bound them up, wrote of the emperor's worst lewdnesses, detailing the acts and the participants, sent the manuscript to Nero, then removed the bindings.

Sapere aude 'dare to be wise'. See under Mottos below at page 68 below.

Satius est impunitum relinqui facinus nocentis quam innocentem damnari 'it is better that the misdeeds of the guilty go unpunished than that an innocent man be condemned'. Ulpian who, with Papinian, was one of two of the great names among Roman jurists. It was however sometimes dangerous to pronounce upon the law. Ulpian was assassinated by the praetorian guard in 228 and Papinian was put to death in 212 for refusing to justify the emperor Caracalla's murder of his brother Geta.

Many who have done jury service, may, in connection with the required burden and standard of proof, have heard it said: 'better that the guilty go free than that the innocent be punished'.

A fascinating example of this view is to be found at Genesis 18 23-33 where God was proposing the destruction of Sodom and Gomorrah on account of the iniquity of its inhabitants. Abraham had to intercede and remind God that some inhabitants were 'righteous'. What was to be their fate and how many such innocents must there be to stave off the destruction proposed? The discussion is remarkable in an area where one might have expected God to have anticipated the problem and to know or at least to have considered the justice.

The British are not familiar with arbitrary arrest and long detention without charge or trial. They refer vaguely but confidently to Magna Carta as custodian of the liberty they have enjoyed and take for granted. Less and less, as they invite the courts to investigate and adjudicate upon the legality of their detention, will they find any protection in the provisions of that charter.

Since the devastating terrorist attack in America on 11th September 2001 the British government has sought to protect its citizens from imminent terrorist threat by legislation containing oppressive measures purporting to maintain security and uphold democracy. Aristotle said that 'the fundamental of democracy is liberty'. Can we protect society by undermining those laws preserving us from arbitrary arrest and detention? Laws so worth defending, which people do not appreciate or sufficiently value, and which, once dismantled are very hard to restore.

It is not possible here to analyse the provisions of the Anti-Terrorism, Crime and Security Act 2001 and the Prevention of Terrorism Act 2005, all following the Terrorism Act 2000. They contain far reaching curbs on the liberty of the citizen (some of which might have been declared unconstitutional if we had a written constitution) and shift in certain areas the power to detain from the judiciary to the executive, a power sometimes exercised on the basis of evidence supplied from abroad and obtained even by torture. Notwithstanding the provisions of these Acts there was in July 2005 still an appalling terrorist attack in London and on 30th June 2007 a car firebomb attack at Glasgow airport and a car bomb attack in London were only just averted.

Might we be heading for a Kafkaesque state where a *geheimnis Staats Polizei* (a secret State police, a Gestapo) knocks on our door at dead of night and escorts us away to disappear? How akin to terrorism is 'any act contrary to the interests of the state'? . . . the ultimate indefinable all embracing reason for which anyone overtly critical of government might be detained. That this is the direction in which we travel was evidenced by the forcible removal and detention of Mr. Walter Wolfgang from the New

Labour party conference for heckling the then Foreign Secretary, Jack Straw. This was done under the anti-terrorist provisions! It attracted much apology: but how many would have noticed or appreciated the potential if the incident had been less high profile and had not involved an old man?

Not satisfied, in November 2005, the Government introduced a Terrorism Bill. *Inter alia* this proposed offences related to terrorism (glorifying, exalting or celebrating any terrorist act, encouraging terrorism, offering terrorist training, acts preparatory to terrorism) offences of questionable necessity, often hard to define, arguably counter-productive and endangering reasonable freedom of speech (see David Pannick in The Times Law 22nd November 2005) and most alarmingly sought to extend from 14 to 90 days the period for which an arrested terrorist suspect might be held without charge. The House of Commons settled for 28 days with access to a High Court Judge for review every 7 days. Was any increase really necessary or sensible?

Protection of the citizen from the terrorist is a commendable objective. But what price should be paid in this land described by Lord Tennyson as: 'of just and old renown where freedom broadens slowly down from precedent to precedent'? There are men in high places urging still increase further to 90 days: from Christmas to Easter, a long time. Are these measures not too great a restriction of our liberties, too dangerous, constituting the thin end of a very sinister wedge?

On 9th November 2005 in The House of Commons the then Prime Minister, Tony Blair, reacted waspishly, "did I hear the right honourable gentleman say 'police state?'" To many the right honourable gentleman's observation was quite in order. It is as well to remember that on February 4th 1933 Hermann Goering, as president of the German Reichstag, introduced a 90 day detention without charge or trial law as part of a decree for the protection of the German People . . *satius est impunitum relinqui facinus nocentis quam innocentem damnari.*

Usque conabor 'I shall continue to strive as best I can'. Old school motto of the Prime Minister, Gordon Brown; Kirkcaldy High School. On 27th June 2007, outside number ten Downing Street, in his first speech as Prime Minister, he announced: "On this day I remember words that have stayed with me since my childhood and which matter a great deal today; my school motto . . ." He did not offer the Latin but gave as translation: 'I will try my utmost'. Perhaps he did not remember it. In September 1995 he presided over a Treasury in which use of Latin tags was abandoned.

Vincit veritas 'truth wins (conquers)'. Useful Latin for governments to know. They should beware of other more easily followed advice. *Fallere fictis utilius quam veritate suadere* 'it is of more use to deceive by falsehoods than to persuade by truth'. *Magna (est) veritas et prevaelebit* 'great is truth and it shall prevail' Apocrypha I Esdras 4.41: this, together with *vincit veritas,* should perhaps join *fortis est veritas* and also be inscribed under Big Ben. See *Dominus illuminatio mea* under Mottos at page 66 below.

Vixi liber et moriar 'I have lived a freeman and will die one.' But *sed quaere* 'but question' as to *et moriar*. See under Mottos below at page 70.

Vox populi 'the voice of the people'. Public sentiment. Reflected in opinion polls. Very influential apparently during the Autumn of 2007 when, folowing the Conservative Party Conference, where very popular promises were made concerning inheritance tax, the New Labour Prime Minister, Gordon

Brown, decided not to call an expected general election and ,
shortly after, his Chancellor of the exchequer proposed changes
greatly lessening the impact of this tax. Abbreviated to '*vox pop*'
it is used in English as a noun, meaning majority public opinion.
Often used to describe street interviews.

GENERAL/MISCELLANEA

Some entries appearing under this head are not entirely serious.

Anobium pertinax. Classificatory name for the Death Watch Beetle. Lives in wood, which it eats creating tunnels terribly destructive of old, particularly walnut, furniture. As one such modern worm larva said to another: "I'm in computers nowadays. How about you?" "I'm afraid I'm still in antique furniture." At breeding time the beetle attracts a mate by a very distinct and audible knocking noise made by banging his/her head against the walls of the tunnel. The superstitious take this as a portent of impending death, hence *Death* Watch Beetle.

Aqua vitae 'water of life'. Euphemism for hard drink, especially whisky and brandy. The Gaelic for water of life *is uisge beatha*, which in the 18th century was corrupted to 'usky' and then to whisky.

Exercitatio Anatomica de Motu Cordis et Sanguinis in Animalibus 'anatomical exercise (treatise) concerning the movement of the heart and blood in animals'. Name of the treatise by an English physician, William Harvey (1578-1657), in which he demonstrated that in the bodies of animals blood did not ebb and flow, as had hitherto been thought, but was pumped round by a muscle, the heart. He was born in Folkestone and a modern hospital at Ashford in Kent is named after him.

Habilis qui hoc signum legit sed nimium propinquus adest 'he is a clever fellow who can read (and understand) this notice but he is coming much too close'. Esoteric advice given by written notice on the rear of a motor car in lettering of the appropriate size to those driving behind.

Hocus-pocus. An anti-Catholic corruption of *hoc est corpus (meum)* 'this is my body'. Offensive contention that the belief that the bread and wine of the Eucharist are converted into the body and blood of Christ at consecration (transubstantiation) is nonsense. *Hocus-pocus* has become a quasi-Latin expression used by conjurers to indicate the operation of some bogus magic. Used too generally to describe actions which involve jiggery-pokery or suggest some magical influence. Compare *abracadabra* another 'magic' word of Roman-Greek origin.

Horas non numero nisi serenas 'I do not show (number) the hours unless they be shining'. Sundials frequently attract Latin inscription. This is a common one recording the actuality.

Iti sapis spotanda tinone. Try and translate that. You will not succeed! Try deciphering. If you still fail, read in English as: 'it is a piss pot and a tin one!' Inscription found on a metal vessel. Another version substitutes *'bigone'* for *'tinone'*.

Moriar si vera non loquor 'may I die if I am not speaking the truth'. Cicero. "As God is my witness I tell the truth" was the declaration of many a witness in the courts. 'He's not, I am, and you don't' is the supposed facetious judicial response. In the infamous trial before the notorious Judge Jeffreys, at the bloody assizes in 1685, of Lady Alice Lisle for allegedly harbouring two pathetic wretches fleeing after the battle of Sedgemoor, a witness (whose evidence did not go to guilt) maintained "My Lord I tell the truth". Before a jury Jeffreys responded: " . . . you are a prevaricating, lying, snivelling rascal".

Nihil illegitimis carborundum est. Pseudo–Latin apparently perhaps meaning 'nothing is by the illegitimate ones meet to be ground down' but understood as 'don't let the bastards grind you down'. The word carborundum does not exist in Latin but looks as if it might: Carborundum, known in 2007 as a grinding abrasive, serves nicely as a bogus Latin word.

Obile heres ago fortibus es in ero Many have been baffled by this. Try to translate it. You will not succeed for it is untranslate-able. Try to decipher. It is joke Latin. Read (nearly!) as: 'Oh Billy, here go forty buses in a row' It is from 'Goodbye Mr. Chips' James Hilton 1900–1954.

Olim quod vulpes aegroto cauta leoni
Respondit referam: quia me vestigia terrent,
Omnia in adversum spectantia, nulla retrorsum.

'Let me refer you to what a cautious fox once said to a sick lion: "Because those footmarks terrify me, all pointing towards you none coming back"'. Horace Epistles I:I:73.

"What big teeth you have grandmamma"!
   Cf, *lupus in fabula* 'wolf in the story'. Terence, Adel. 1.21.

Not a Roman Little Red Riding Hood equivalent: rather used of one spoken of, who just happens to appear. Speak of the devil!

Opus artificem probat 'the work proves the craftsman'. A craftsman will be known by the standard or quality of his work. The word *fecit* 'he made,' followed by a name, is often used to identify the maker of some object (a piece of furniture or pottery). Likewise with artists on paintings may apppear *pinxit* 'he painted'. Some artistic creators of beautiful things are loathe to part with them and so reserve a little something to themselves with the words *salus factori* '(good) health to the maker'.

Qui nunc it per iter tenebricosum
Illuc unde negant redire quemquam.
'who now goes along the dark road, whence it is said no one returns'. Catullus

Compare:

> 'But that the dread of something after death,–
> The undiscover'd country, from whose bourn
> No traveller returns, ...'
>> William Shakespeare. Hamlet Act 3.1.

And only vaguely comparable:

> 'Like one that on a lonesome road
> Doth walk in fear and dread,
> And having once turned round walks on,
> Because he knows a frightful fiend
> Doth close behind him tread'.
>> Samuel Taylor Coleridge 1772-1834.
>> The Rime of the Ancient Mariner.

Sine qua non 'without which not'. A fundamental or essential. Food is a 'without which not' of life. The expression appears in the Compact Oxford Dictionary and so may be regarded as co-opted and part of the English language. It is nice to know that the three Latin words each mean, literally, without, which and not.

Tabula (in) naufragio 'plank in a shipwreck'. Whatever, in a crisis, one can find to latch onto that saves the day. In the case of shipwreck, when there is a plank sufficient to keep only one man afloat and two grab hold of it, does the one who pushes the other off to his doom, and thereby saves himself, commit murder? The word *naufragia* was used also to describe the crashes at great speed in Rome's chariot races (eg., at the *Circus Maximus* in Rome), the excitement and carnage of which more Romans found entertaining than even the gladiatorial contests at the Colosseum. The charioteers were the pin-up boys of the times and, like top footballers, became extremely rich but often lived only a short time in which to enjoy it.

Veredus 'a swift or running horse'. If at the races you find entered a horse of this name, it might just be worth a sizeable bet.

Virus 'a liquid poison, a snake venom'. In English virus means a minute organism capable of causing disease and sometimes death in humans and animals. Different only in detail. *Venenum* is another word for poison or anything noxious.

EPITAPHS

Epitaphs are words written in memory of a deceased person, usually as an inscription on a plaque or on a tombstone. William Camden (1551–1629 historian and sometime headmaster of Westminster School, who published in 1660 a list of the epitaphs in Westminster Abbey) considered that an epitaph should show 'love to the deceased, memory to posterity and comfort to friends'. Dr. Samuel Johnson (1709 – 1784) expressed further strong views on the subject. He noted that 'in lapidary inscriptions a man is not upon oath' (note *de mortuis nil nisi* below) and contended that 'the language of the country of which a man was a native is not the language fit for his epitaph', which should be 'in ancient and permanent language' hence his famous outburst in relation to the epitaph of Oliver Goldsmith, which he (Johnson) wrote (for which see *'nullum quod tetigit non ornavit'* below).

Many epitaphs on gravestones, especially the older ones, are written in Latin. Thus on too many their message is lost. For the enterprising and the determined, however, help is at hand in the form of an instructive little book entitled 'Reading Latin Epitaphs – A Handbook for Beginners' by John Parker. Three extracts are reproduced and follow on pages 53–57 below. Translation may however prove to be only part of the battle. Many tombstone inscriptions are to be found obliterated by lichen, moss and the ravages of time, and it may be necessary to labour mightily first even to read the lettering. On some Latin epitaphs remember that the letter V is the modern U and sometimes the letter I will appear where it should be read as J (since there was no letter J in the Latin alphabet). Translation may then bring about a wish to know far more about the one whose remains lie beneath than is to be learned from the few words set in stone; something borne out perhaps by the above mentioned extracts from John Parker's book and by *Carino Civi Rom* below. Further fascinating research may be in prospect.

Beatae memoriae 'of blessed memory.' Words often seen on tombstones and on memorial plaques.'

Carino
  Civi Rom
  Ann.L
  Rufinus.et Carina.et Avita.
  Fil.I.Eius et. Romana. Uxor

'(in memory of) *Carinus*, Roman citizen, (died) aged 50. His children, *Rufinus, Carina* and *Avita* with his wife *Romana* (arranged for his memorial).' Inscription on a Roman tombstone found in 1907 built into the porch of St. George's, Fordington in Dorset: beautiful Roman lettering skilfully cut and well preserved. *Carinus* was a Roman citizen and a man probably of some importance but nothing further is known about him than the names of his wife and three children. Unless very famous or distinguished, we should all write our autobiographies if, after we are gone, we wish anything to be known of our life on this earth. So few children know much about their parents' lives and too often, when they reach an age when this is of interest, find that they have left it too late to ask.

De mortuis nil (nihil) nisi bonum (bene) 'concerning the dead nothing unless it be good'. Don't speak ill of the dead. Not an epitaph as such but appropriate here. Taken with Dr. Johnson's observation (above) that those writing epitaphs are not upon oath, this admonition (the Latin taken from a Greek saying) perhaps warns against accepting too readily the eulogies that are to be found. The directive may too be a reflection of the procedure urged by the legal maxim *audi alteram partem* 'let the other party be heard', a canon of natural justice. The dead are not there to be heard in their own defence. To speak against them in their absence would be an injustice. The maxim (as it is in the law but emanates from St. Augustine's *De Duabus Animabus* xiv.2 where he insists that to every question there are two sides) may however be largely unnecessary for:

> 'The evil that men do lives after them;
> The good is oft interred with their bones.'

> William Shakespeare
> Julius Caesar. Act III Sc.2 ll 81-82.

Finis 'the end'. In one sense the word is an epitaph for atheists only. For all it is the end of this life. The question is whether anything comparable lies beyond. 'Death is part of the future for everyone. It is the last post of this life and the reveille of the next. Everywhere men fear death. It is the end of our present life, it is the parting from loved ones, it is the setting out into the unknown'. Pope John XXIII. Lucretius (c. 99 - c 55BC) observed: *vitaque mancipio, nulli datur, omnibus usu* 'and life free-hold to nobody is given, it is for all leasehold'.

Hic iacet 'here lies'. To be found on tombstones followed by the name of the dead person.

Hic sepultus (situs) est 'here is buried (situated)'. An abbreviation of either form is HSE, at least on Roman epitaphs from the first century.

Hodie adest, cras aberit 'here today gone tomorrow'.

Hodie mihi cras tibi 'to me today, to you tomorrow'. Seen on old gravestones. A message with a certain compelling inevitability. But applicable in life as well as to death. If you suffer a setback and suspect another of schadenfreude, just think, life is unpredictable and don't worry because *hodie mihi* but probably *cras tibi*. Cf., *quod sum eris* below.

Incisa notis marmora publicis per quae spiritus et vita redit bonis post mortem ducibus 'marble graves inscribed with public records whereby breath and life return to worthy heroes after death'. Horace Odes 4.8. 13-15.

In memoriam 'in memory (of)'. To the memory of a dead person.

Natus 'born'. Tombstones sometimes record lifespan by reference to date *natus* and that *obit*. See below.

Nullum quod tetigit non ornavit 'he touched nothing which he did not adorn'. Part of Dr. Samuel Johnson's epitaph written for Oliver Goldsmith (c. 1776). There were those not happy with this and a deputation of luminaries headed by Sir Joshua Reynolds made proposals for other versions written in English.

Johnson resisted their overtures and announced finally "that nothing would induce him to disgrace the walls of Westminster Abbey with an inscription in English".

Obit 'he/she died.' To be found on tombstones and church records with the date of his/her death.

Quod sum eris 'what I am you will be'. Epitaph on a Roman gravestone. Cf., *hodie adsit cras absit* and *hodie mihi cras tibi* above. Speaks to inevitable fact. But perhaps an accolade from a grandee to an admirably industrious and able young man or woman.

Resurgam 'I shall rise again'. During demolition of the old St. Paul's (c. 1670), Sir Christopher Wren came across a broken gravestone with the word *'resurgam'* engraved upon it. He took this as an omen that his ambitious ideas for the building of a new St. Paul's Cathedral would come to fruition, as indeed they did. Better known is the inscription on his tomb in the new St. Paul's Cathedral acknowledging his illustrious architectural career: *Si monumentum requiris, circumspice* 'if you seek a monument (to him) look around you'.

RIP Usually taken as an abbreviation of 'rest in peace' but in fact the English reflects the earlier Latin *requiescat in pace* 'may he (or she) rest in peace'. To be seen on many gravestones.

Scottorum malleus 'hammer of the Scots'. Remarkable as an epitaph. See under Holiday/Tourism at page 31 above.

Sta viator: amabilem conjugem calcas 'pause traveller, for you tread upon a beloved wife.' Epitaph on the grave of Emma

Bovary in Gustave Flaubert's novel 'Madame Bovary' (1857). Emma had committed suicide after an adulterous episode. *Siste, viator* 'stop, traveller' was a fairly common inscription on Roman tombstones.

Viriditas 'greenness, liveliness, freshness'. Latin word associated with the head and face of a man from which various fruit, flowers or foliage are seen to be growing. Cut in stone and decorating Roman tombs in the first century, these have become known as 'The Green Man'. Norman masons introduced him to England after Duke William's Conquest in 1066. He has continued to pop up ever since and despite destruction of many at the Reformation, quite a few survive and he is to be found (sometimes apparently hidden) on tombstones, on memorials, on walls, in title pages of early printed books etc. The earliest example of a Green Man in a church is at Trier Cathedral in Germany (he was brought from a Roman Temple and built into a pillar). There are many theories but his meaning or significance remains unknown. The delightful medieval story of Sir Gawain and the Green Knight is clearly a part of the Green Man mystery.

There follow three extracts form 'Reading Latin Epitaphs A Handbook for Beginners' reproduced by kind courtesy of the author, John Parker.

Tavistock

HONORATÆ SACRUM MEMORIÆ
IOHAÑIS GLANVIL HVIVS QVONDAM
IVSTICIARIORVM DE COMMVNI
BANCO: QVI MERITV FACTVS IVDEX
SVMO CVM LABORE ADMINISTRAVIT

IVSTITIAM, IVSTITIA CONSERVAVIT
PACEM, PACE EXPECTAVIT MORTEM,
ET MORTE INVENIT REQVIEM 27
DIE JVLII ANNO DOM 1600

Sacred to the honoured memory of John Glanvil of this [town] formerly of the Justices of the Common Bench, who, appointed a judge on his merits, administered justice with the utmost energy, by justice conserved the peace, in peace awaited death, and by death found rest on 27th July A.D. 1600.

Notes

Memoriæ "To the memory" dative singular of *memoria*.

Meritu "Deservedly, by merit". This should be *merito*, an adverb derived from the ablative of meritum, a second declension noun.

Sumo cum labore *Sumo* is an abbreviation of *summo*. The phrase shows the regular order of adjective+preposition+noun.

Administravit...conservavit...expectavit...invenit All are third person singular perfect indicative of their respective verbs; *administro, conservo ex(s)pecto, invenio*.

Requiem The accusative singular of *requies*. This can mean either "rest" or "a resting place".

St. John's, Exeter

M.S. Chester Henrici Macmullen, scholæ Exoniensis alumni, Stephani Macmullen M.D. de Bridgewater in Comitatu Somerset filii natu maximi moribus

egregiis ingenioque præstantissimo juvenis quem
optimarum artium doctrinæque appetentissimum
abstulit mors immatura die 18 Novembris 1824, anno
æt 15. Quis desiderio sit pudor, aut modus tam cari
capitis?

Sacred to the memory of Chester Henry MacMullen, a pupil of
Exeter School, eldest son of Stephan Macmullen, M. D., of
Bridgewater in the county of Somerset; a youth of noble conduct
and of most outstanding talents, whom untimely death tore away
from the most assiduous study of the best of art and learning on
18th November 1824, aged 15. "What shame or limit should
there be in grieving for one so dear?"

Notes

Henrici The genitive of *Henricus*, the Latin form of "Henry".

M.D. *Medicinæ Doctor*, "Doctor of Medicinte".

Appetentissimum Literally "most desiring, most seeking
after", describing the boy himself (*quem*).

Abstulit The third person singular perfect indicative of *aufero*,
"I carry off".

Quis...capitis The frequently-quoted opening sentence of one
of Horace's Odes (Book 1, xxiv). *Sit*, "it may be", is the third
person singular present subjunctive of *sum*, "I am". *Tam carii
capitis* is literally "of such a dear head", with *capitis*, the genitive
singular of *caput*, "a head", standing (by synecdoche) simply for
"person".

St. Saviour's, Dartmouth

> Memoriæ Sacrum
> Rogeri Vavasor Qui fortiter
> Se defendendo, & publico Patriæ
> Inimico oppugnando magnanimæ
> Succubuit Morti
> Vicesimo octavo Die Mensis Martij
> > Dom 1696
> Anno
> > Ætat 34
> Et
> Iuxta hunc Locum
> Conduntur Reliquiæ
> Henrici Vavasor Filii
> Vnici Rogeri supradicti
> Spe Resurrectionis Generalis
> Qui
> Obiit secundo Die Mensis Sept
> > Dom 1727
> Anno
> > Ætat 36

Sacred to the memory of Roger Vavasour who, bravely defending himself and attacking the common enemy of the Fatherland succumbed to a hero's death on 28th March 1696, aged 34.

And next to this place are interred in hope of general resurrection the remains of Henry Vavasour, only son of the above-named Roger, who died on 2nd December 1727, aged 36.

Notes

Se defendendo Literally "in defending himself". Although *defendendo* is ablative, *se* is not ablative but accusative, and so this is not an ablative absolute construction.

Publico...inimico oppugnando Again not an ablative absolute.

Succubuit The third person singular perfect indicative of *succumbo*, "I succumb".

Anno Dom...Ætat An example of economy of writing, where *Anno* serves both *Dom(ini)* and *Ætat(is)*.

Conduntur The third person plural present passive indicative of *condo*, "I preserve, bury".

Who was the 'common enemy' in 1696? France, in conflict with Britain, Holland and some German States.

SOCIAL

There is abundant wisdom to be derived from reading what was written in Latin so many years ago. Below is set out just a little.

Adulescentem verecundum esse debet 'a young man ought to be modest'. Plautus. Why not older men too? Cicero (the great orator, lawyer, writer and statesman 106-43 BC) was aged 43 when he became consul (which he achieved at the earliest date permitted by the constitution at the time and despite the absence of advantage from birth: he was a *novus homo* 'a new man', arriviste) after which he made the remarkable famous claim: '*o fortunatam natam me consule Romam* 'o happy Rome, born in my consulship.' He was scarcely a modest man but, possessed of such undeniably great ability and talent, that it was perhaps very difficult for him to be or to appear modest.

Advocatus diaboli 'Advocate of the devil . . . devil's advocate'. The name given to an official appointed by the Roman Catholic Church, whose duty was to put the case against a proposed beatification or canonisation and to oppose the *promotor fidei*, the promotor of the faith, his opposite number. These offices were abolished in 1983 by Pope John Paul II and an investigative procedure replaced the adversarial. The expression *advocatus diaboli* in common usage has come to refer to one who advocates an opposite viewpoint and who often argues for the sake of argument, the unpopular, the absurd or the unarguable.

Benedictus benedicat 'may the blessed Lord bless (our meal)'. A short form of Latin grace the meaning of which is known to too few. Sometimes after the meal is said '*Benedicto benedicatur*' 'may blessing be given to the Blessed Lord'.

Dum vivimus vivamus 'while we live let us live' Epicurean motto. Cf.,

> *Ille potens sui*
> *laetusque deget. Cui licet in diem*
> *dixisse vixi cras vel atra*
> *nube polum pater occupato*
> *vel sole puro.*

> 'Happy the man and happy he alone,
> He, who can call today his own:
> He, who secure within, can say
> Tomorrow do thy worst, for I have lived today'.

> Horace, Odes 3.29 lines 41-45.
> Translation John Dryden 1631-1700.

Eheu fugaces labuntur anni 'alas the fleeting years slip by'. Famous line of Horace (Odes II xiv. 1-2). Lament of the ageing, but useful for greeting old friends long absent. The above quotation omits the twice repeated name of the person (one *Postumus*) to whom this was addressed in Horace's original (it makes for confusion).

Ex his omnibus longe sunt humanissimi qui Cantium incolant 'the inhabitants of Kent are the most civilised of all these (Britons)'. Caesar, *Commentariii*. Gallic War v.14. Essential entry from an author living in Kent.

Fertilior seges est alienis semper in agris 'corn is always more fruitful (abundant) when in the fields of others'. Ovid. The grass is always greener on the other side. Those with more than one dog will understand the analogous proposition 'the same food tastes different and better in another's bowl'. Those without a dog should know that a dog will often eat with enthusiasm from another's bowl exactly what he has just left in his own. *Canis in praesepi* 'dog in a manger'. The dog which denies hay to the oxen, which he cannot eat himself.

Festina lente 'hurry slowly'. More haste, less speed is the English equivalent. To be heeded in particular by retired gardeners. Too fierce an attack on the overwhelming growth of mid-summer will almost certainly result in painful dysfunction of some ageing limb (usually the back) and will set the whole project seriously back.

Fortiter in re suaviter in modo 'strong in deed gentle in manner'. Sometimes (as on page 70 below) rendered as *suaviter in modo fortiter in re*. What a civilised nation we would be if all citizens could be so described. Particularly important for judges.

Horresco referens ' I am afraid as I relate' (I shudder to mention it). Your best friend wouldn't!

Integer vitae scelerisque purus 'clean living (blameless in life) and free of vice). Famous statement from Horace's Odes quoted in E.M.Forster's 'The Longest Journey'. How many politicians (or any of us for that matter !) could properly be so described?

In vino veritas 'in wine the truth'. Drinking wine so lowers the barriers of inhibition and caution that the truth, and so much else that may be indiscreet, will out. Take care with drink if you don't want to make a lot of trouble for yourself. Remember Horace *nescit vox missa reverti* 'a word once uttered cannot be recalled'. (Ars Poetica 390): he was in fact suggesting that authors should hold back their work for nine years before publication! Only that time is sufficient for proper reflection and revision.

Juveniscimus stercus legendo 'by shifting dung we become young (shifting dung keeps you young)'. An adage maintained by those devoted to horses and who manually clear their pastures every day. Others, forced to stand in from time to time, agree that it really ought to have this effect as compensation, because a greater waste of life can scarcely be imagined. *Quid de utilitate loquar de stercorandi?* 'what shall I say about the usefulness of spreading dung?' Cicero, De Senectute, XV, 54.

Libenter enim sufferes insipientes cum sitis ipsi sapientes 'for ye suffer fools gladly seeing you yourselves are wise.' Vulgate St. Paul Epistle to the Corinthians II.ii.19. There are those who pride themselves on not suffering fools gladly. Of course there are fools and stupid fools: the latter ought perhaps not readily to be tolerated. Was it despicable to laugh at the Deputy Prime Minister, John Prescott, when he announced himself glad to be back on *terracotta* (brownish red earthenware, unglazed), when perhaps he intended *terra firma?* (dry land). There is ample warning: 'Be not wise in your own conceits.'

Romans 12.16. and 'The fool doth think that he is wise, but the wise man knows himself to be a fool.' William Shakespeare As You Like It. Act V Sc.1.l. 34. and *sapere aude* 'dare to be wise'. Horace Epist.' I.II.40. A telling piece of verse written by Dorothy Wordsworth (sister of William) 1771-1855 is apposite:

> 'If all good people were clever,
> And all clever people were good,
> The world would be nicer than ever
> We thought that it possibly could.
>
> But somehow, 'tis seldom or never
> The two hit it off as they should;
> The good are so harsh to the clever,
> The clever so rude to the good.'

Nihil est quod decet quam constantia 'nothing is as becoming as constancy'. Cicero. One who is constant is one who is unchanging, faithful and dependable. Constancy is a word too little in evidence in 2007 as the divorce rate soars and too many fear the responsibilities inherent in old-fashioned marriage.

Nolite fumare See under AD 2007 at page 21 above.

Nulli malum pro malo reddentes 'render unto no man evil for evil'. Vulgate Romans 12:17.
Failure to heed this edict is to descend to the same base level as the doer of evil. Getting your own back is not in the longer term as satisfactory as it may initially have appeared. Telling example is to be found in Alexander Dumas's Count of Monte Cristo. See too under Ecclesiastical and Biblical at page 89 below.

Nunc est bibendum 'now is the time to drink'. Not a Roman six o'clock observation. From Horace Odes LXXXVII.1 written in celebration of the downfall of Cleopatra. *Nunc bibamus* 'now let us drink' is more immediate.

Opus Dei 'work of God'. The name of a lay Roman Catholic religious order. It was founded in Spain in 1928 by a cleric, Jose Maria Escriva de Balaguer, with the declared objective of maintaining Christian ideals by the example of its members. Controversial and semi-secret, it gained considerable power and influence through an élite membership in General Franco's Spain of the 1960s. Balaguer died in 1975 and was canonised in 2002. There was a member of Opus Dei in the UK Government of 2007. The Order features prominently in Dan Brown's 'The Da Vinci Code' where it is innacurately portrayed (it is a lay order and has no monks) and disgracefully seen as being very sinister. Read 'The Da Vinci Code and the Secrets of the Temple, by Robin Griffith-Jones, The Master of the Temple. Canterbury Press 2006.

Quam pulchra es 'how beautiful thou art' (familiar form). Name of a three-part motet written by a young King Henry VIII and one of his thirty four surviving compositions. Be careful if you talk about it. A lady of uncertain years and undeniably unhappy appearance talking music with a young man did not hear the Latin but was surprised, and far from amused, to hear just the English.

Quomodo vales 'how are you keeping?' A greeting too readily used. Those with terminal or progressive illness do not always appreciate the question. To be used with care and discretion.

Totum in eo est ut tibi imperes 'what it all comes to is that you should take control of yourself. Cicero.Tusculanae Disputationes. Good counsel for the hot tempered, the promiscuous, the smoker and the binge drinker. Advice also of the robust 'pull yourself together' school.

Ut amem et foveam 'that I should love and cherish'. A tattoo of David Beckham. Another is *perfecto in spiritu* 'perfect in spirit'. Is Latin again fashionable? And in 2007 might Latin and Latin mottos take America by storm with David Beckham and Posh?

Vir sapit qui pauca loquitur 'he is a wise man who says little.' There is too a *tempus tacendi et tempus loquendi* 'a time to be silent and a time to speak.' Vulgate Ecclesiastes 3.7. Remember too *nescit vox missa reverti* (under *in vino veritas* above*)* 'a word once uttered cannot be recalled.' *Magna res est vocis et silenti temperamentum* 'the great thing is a right balance between talking and silence'. Seneca the younger attributed Proverbs 74. Confucius' Analects observe: 'For one word a man is often deemed to be wise, and for one word he is often deemed to be foolish. We should be careful indeed what we say.' It is clearly very dangerous to open one's mouth at all! No sooner do I open my mouth than I put my foot in it! See *nescis mi fili, quantilla prudentia mundus regatur* under Political at page 35 above.

MOTTOS

VIXI LIBER ET MORIAR

Short sentences or phrases stating a belief, an ideal or an objective: generally honourable, idealistic, brave and/or worthy. Many of their sentiments much needed today. Often representative of a person, family or institution and sometimes an integral part of a coat of arms.

Alta pete 'aspire to high things, aim high'. Try not to settle for second best. In relation to career that does not necessarily mean that the making of money should be paramount.

Audio, video, disco 'I hear, I see, I learn'. A good prima facie motto for life but regrettably the third word does not on the whole apply to the results of much of what we see and hear on the television.

Aut agere aut mori 'either to do or die'. All or nothing?

Citius, altius, fortius 'faster, higher, stronger (braver?). The Olympic Motto, known to too few. Remember for 2012.

Deo fidimus 'in God we trust'. A well known motto under attack currently as God's existence is boldly queried. Professor Richard Dawkins, in his book 'The God Delusion', would have it that all those who do not delude themselves ought to be atheists. John Humphrys in his more recent book 'In God we Doubt' (*Deo diffidimus* or *dubitamus*) looks for God but ends up agnostic. However the powers that be seem to be loyal still to belief involving a leap of faith: see the Latin inscription *tueatur unita Deus* on the 2007 £5 crown coin reproduced in part on the front of the jacket of this book and in full at page iii above. See too under AD 2007 at page 24 above. How many can recite every word of the Apostle's Creed with a clear conscience?

Domine dirige nos 'guide us o Lord'. Motto of the City of London. Does God really guide all those sharp financiers and insider dealers?

Dominus illuminatio mea 'the Lord is my light'. From Psalm 27.1 (26.1 for the Latin in the Vulgate). This is the motto of Oxford University. The words which follow are less well known: *et salus mea quem timebo*? 'and my safety, whom then shall I fear? An historic motto of the City of Oxford is *fortis est veritas* 'truth is good': the words are inscribed under the clock on Carfax Tower in the centre of the town: the same words should be inscribed under Big Ben for all to see and heed.

Dum vivimus vivamus 'while we live let us live'. See under Social at page 59 above.

Est modus in rebus 'there is a right proportion in things' Horace Satires I.i.106. Moderation in all things.

Hinc lucem et pocula sacra 'from this source (springs) light and sacred draughts (of learning)'. Motto of Cambridge University.

Hostis honori invidia 'envy (is) the enemy of honour'. A country general practitioner once observed, when visiting one with real troubles: "you look around and feel that everybody else is 'alright Jack'. But when you have practised medicine as long as I have, you will realise that nearly everyone has some unhappy burden somewhere dragging them down".

In hoc scuto fidemus 'in this shield we trust'. See *scutum* below at page 108 and *testudo* under Military and Naval below.

Nihil sine Deo 'nothing without God' Sometimes *sine Deo nihil*. Certainly neither of these forms is the motto of Professor Richard Dawkins.

Nullius in verba 'on the words of nobody.' Mottto of the Royal Society. Less literally but meaningfully translated variously as: 'taking nobody's word for it' 'taking nothing on trust' 'only by satisfying oneself' 'reliant upon no other'. CF., *nullius addictus jurare in verba magister* 'bound to swear to the words of no master' Horace Epist 1.i.xiv.

Paulatim ergo certe 'little by little therefore (but) surely'. Not a motto for today where technology speeds up everything and nobody writes a letter any more: making do with a gabbled fax or e-mail. Act in haste repent at leisure. Note *festina lente* (see under Social above), a favourite saying of the Emperor Augustus, and *tarde sed tute* 'slow but sure'.

Persuasionem appetens quam veritatem 'seeking (desirous of) persuasion (rather) than truth' and *suave malit audire plebs quam scire* 'people will prefer to hear what is agreeable than to know the truth. On this basis how much is readily kept from us? (radioactive leaks, poisoned water supplies?). Not mottos but advices conveniently made use of (consciously or unconsciously) by those who govern us. Why it is important that *veritas vincit* 'truth wins (conquers)'.

Quo fas et gloria ducunt 'where right and glory lead'. Motto of The Royal Engineers Corps.

Sapere aude 'dare to be wise'. Claimed as a motto by many. The expression originates from Horace's Epistles (I:ii.40), where the poet exhorts one Lollius Maximus to mend his ways and not to delay. 'The fool doth think that he is wise, but the wise man doth know himself to be a fool'. William Shakespeare. As You Like It. Act 5 Sc. I. l. 34.

Semper eadem 'always the same'. Motto of Queen Elizabeth I. She was an accomplished classicist.

Semper paratus 'always ready'. The Latin language caters for all states of readiness or unreadiness. So: *Nunquam non paratus* 'never not ready' (a more verbose form of *semper paratus*). *In omnia paratus* 'ready for everything'. *Ad utrumque paratus* 'ready for either case or event'. *Nunquam paratus* 'never ready'!

Sine Deo nihil 'without God nothing'. See *nihil sine Deo* above.

Sit sine labe decus 'let my honour be without stain'. There are quite a lot of mottos related to that decaying and increasingly rare quality, honour. So: *fidem qui perdit nihil pote ultra perdere* 'who loses his honour has nothing more to lose'. Publilius Syrus Sententiae F.14. *Potius mori quam foedari* 'better to die than be disgraced'. Thus the conquered Roman fell on his sword. This may however also have had something to do with the fact that the alternatives for those defeated in war were to become slaves or be put to death. Virgil's famous observation *una salus victis nullam sperare salutem* 'the only safe course for the vanquished is to expect no safety (mercy)' is in point. See under AD2007 above. See too *hostis honori invidia* above

Stet fortuna domus 'may the fortune of the house live long'. Based on Virgil, Georgics. iv. 209, which spoke of a flourishing hive of bees. A loose translation, known to many, is; 'I'm all right Jack'. Translated as 'may the fortune of the school live long' these words serve as the title to one of a number of Harrow School Songs. Of particular interest is a verse written for the visit of an old boy to the school: Sir Winston Churchill in the dark days of 1940.

> 'Nor less we praise in sterner days
>   The leader of our nation.
> And Churchill's name shall win acclaim
>   From each new generation.
> While in this fight to guard the right
>   Our country to defend Sir.
> Here grim and gay we mean to stay,
>   And stick it to the end Sir.'

The word 'gay' must be taken with the meaning of the times, cheerful, carefree, lest criminal activity may seem [also of the times] to be attributed by the words 'grim and gay' leaving an unhappily false picture of the 1940 Harrow schoolboy.

Suaviter in modo fortiter in re 'gentle in manner strong (resolute) in deed'. Most desirable especially for judges. See *fortiter in re . . .* above under Social.

Tibi ipsi esto verus 'to thyself be true'. Inscription on the coat of arms of Patrick Phillips Esq High Sheriff of Buckinghamshire 2004 – 5. *quondam* City of London whizz kid. Preferred very loose translation is 'I did it my way'Cf., *faber est quisque fortunae suae* 'each man is the maker of his own fortune'. Proverb quoted by Sallust De Republica, i.2. and by F.E.Smith, Lord Birkenhead. God helps them who help themselves.

Veritas odit moras 'truth hates delays'. Motto of Arts and Letters Daily (aldaily.com) an organisation which picks the best articles and book reviews from newspapers, politics and the arts. Latin back in fashion?

Virtutis fortuna comes 'fortune is the companion of valour'. Motto of the Duke of Wellington. Both the Duke and Napoleon Buonaparte took with them on campaign a copy of Julius Caesar's *commentarii* 'commentaries' (on the Gallic and Civil wars – *de bello Gallico* and *De Bello Civile*).

Vixi liber et moriar 'I have lived a freeman and will die one'. One of the clan or family mottos associated with the surname 'Gray'. Something which it becomes difficult to expect in a UK, which increasingly can only just be termed a free country. For those living in UK this motto can properly be used only if one believes that at that certain but indeterminate future date of death the UK could accurately be described as a free country. At present it has in place all the surveillance potential and levers of power necessary for a junta to turn it instantly and irretrievably into a totalitarian state. Live each day as though it were your last and one day you will be right: but will you die a free man? See above under Political.

LAW AND JUSTICE

In 1999 there was unleashed an onslaught against the use of
Latin in the law, championed by the Lord Chief Justice, Lord
Woolf, using publication of his new Civil Procedure Rules as a
springboard. A similar attempt had been made before, as long
ago as 1730, when an Act was passed abolishing the use of Law
Latin in legal proceedings. But it proved counter-productive and
such Latin was permitted by another Act two years later. Latin
however is to be found in abundance in old cases to which, in a
system based on precedent, lawyers are bound to refer. Further,
since lord Woolf's retirement the use of legal Latin seems to be
creeping back and is to be found in judgements of the House of
Lords, the highest court in the land. See eg., Harding v
Wealands [2006] UKHL 32. Below are just a very few of the
more common and significant expressions. A wider collection
and often more detailed commentary, is available in John Gray's
Lawyers' Latin, A Vade-Mecum. Robert Hale 2006.

Cui bono? 'to whom good?'. Who profits? Who stands to gain? Famous expression used more than once by Cicero in the Roman courts eg., in Pro Milone 32. Succinct question, the answer to which may be a useful guide, particularly in Criminal cases. Perhaps it is also a useful touchstone for use and guidance in life generally.

Fiat justitia 'let justice be done'. A resoundingly high minded declaration of intent, which used to be the worthy motto of the General Council of the Bar but was superseded in 1999 (when use in the law of Latin became politically incorrect and fell into disfavour) by the English 'justice for all'.
Both were all very well but justice is an indefinable concept, upon which countless factors bear. The Roman Emperor Justinian (in his Institutes, volumes compiled *circa AD* 533 for practical use in learning the law) defined it as 'the constant and perpetual wish to render every one his due'. But what is a man's due? Assuming good laws, is that not for every trial to decide? Something which keeps lawyers in business. But in the end 'Justice and truth are of too fine a quality to be measured by our clumsy human instruments'. Blaise Pascal 1623 – 62.

Fortescue De Laudibus Legum Angliae 'Fortescue in Praise of the Laws of England'. Title of a book printed for and sold by one John Amery at The Peacock near St. Dunstan's Church, Fleetstreet (sic) in 1674. He is to be found quoted in seventeenth century judgements.eg., in The Case Of the Proclamations (1611), 12 Co.Rep.74. A lot of Latin was used. How many lawyers could cope today?

Fundamenta justitiae, primum ut ne cui noceatur, deinde ut communi utilitati serviatur. 'the fundamentals of justice are that no one should suffer wrong and that the public good be served. Cicero De Officiis 1 31. *Sed quaere* ('but question') what in law is a wrong and what exactly serves the public good? This is of prime importance today. Is it wrong to detain a man for 28, 56 or 90 days without charge or trial? Does such action serve the public good in the context of terrorist threat? See *Satius est impunitum* etc., under Political at page 38 above. Cf., *justitia est* below.

Habeas Corpus 'you are to have (or produce) the body'. Name given to a writ requiring a detained person to be brought before the courts of the land so as to determine the lawfulness of his or her detention. Long thought of as the custodian of an Englishman's liberty, its efficacy has been seriously eroded by the anti-terrorist legislation following attack in America on September 11th 2001 and by outrageously one-sided statutory provision for easy extradition at the request of the USA. The nation is dangerously complacent about the potential and direction of travel of these inroads.

It is so hard to turn back the clock. See *satius est impunitum* . . . under Political above.

In pari delicto potior est conditio defendentis 'the position of the defendant is the stronger where both parties are equally villainous'. A villain may invoke the law to press a claim against one whose behaviour in the transaction in question is comparably bad, but the law will be slow to assist him, leaving the defendant in the stronger position. Another resoundingly splendid sounding expression speaks also against wrongdoers. *Omnia praesumuntur contra spoliatorem* 'all is presumed against a wrongdoer'.Thus if one has converted to his own use the chattel of another, then, if he cannot return it in equivalent condition, or cannot prove its value, the court will place upon it the highest possible valuation and will reflect that in the claimant's damages. There was a strange quirk in the presumptions of Roman law. Slave dealers were bound to disclose any serious defects in their ware but were presumed to be rascals and were liable for all serious defects, whether or not they knew of them.

In personam 'against the person'. Rights may be given by the law against the person or against a thing (*in rem*). Rights against a person run the risk that the person may not be good for the money or all of it. Rights against a thing (usually land by mortgage, but sometimes a chattel eg., pawn) do not run so great a risk and are safer.

Justitia est constans et perpetua voluntas jus suum cuique tribuens 'justice is the constant and perpetual wish to render every one his due'. The opening words of Justinian's (Roman Emperor 527-565) Institutes (four volumes which he caused to be compiled for purposes of learning the Law). It does not answer the question, what is a man's due? Cf., *fundamenta justitiae* above. What is a wrong and what is a man's due (very much inter-related) are issues which keep lawyers in constant and perpetual business

Omnia praesumuntur rite esse acta 'all things are presumed to have been correctly done'. A Latin tag reflecting the *prima facie* presumption of the law. Remarkable. Cicero, that most illustrious of lawyers, wrote *cuiusvis hominis est errare* 'it is (the nature) of any man to err'.

Quamdiu se bene gesserint 'so long as they shall have behaved well'. A High Court Judge's continuing tenure in office depends upon his or her behaving well and has done since the Act of Settlement 1701. In much of the 16th century judges held office *durante beneplacito* 'so long as it well pleases (the monarch)'. Under the provisions of the Constitutional Reform Act 2005 an Office for Judicial Complaints was set up in 2006. In July of 2007 the Lord Chief Justice and the Lord Chancellor referred Mr Justice Peter Smith (whose name had come to the public's notice as the trial judge of first instance in the Da Vinci Code plagiarism trial) to this Office for it to consider the Court of Appeal's finding that he had behaved intemperately and shown undoubted animosity towards solicitors with whom he had been personally involved and who had asked him to stand down in a matter brought before him. *Inter alia* it is open to the Office after investigation to recommend reprimand or even dismissal. In case of the latter Parliament would have to be asked to carry out the recommendation. No judge of such seniority has previously been referred to the Office.

Res ipsa loquitur 'the thing itself speaks' literally or 'the thing speaks for itself'. An expression known to a great many who are not lawyers as exemplifying Latin as used in the law. The layman's favourite legal maxim? Translation is far from the whole story and reference books are often misleading. In law the expression means more than that something is quite obvious given a certain fact or facts. In the law relating to the tort (wrong) of negligence, it is for a claimant (plaintiff) to prove that the party against whom he claims was negligent, in breach of a duty of care, which the law deems owed, and that the damage in respect of which he claims has resulted. A barrel falls from the first floor of a warehouse onto the head of a man below, injuring him seriously. The man, as claimant, establishes these facts and matters. The defendant says 'but you haven't shown how the barrel came to fall and how I was negligent'. The law permits the claimant to answer '*res ipsa loquitur*, the warehouse is in your occupation and control, only you can know how the accident came about. It is to be inferred that there was negligence unless and until you can explain and prove that there was not'. The expression is all about who in a trial must prove what and at what point this onus may shift. The Latin expression has probably evolved as a useful term of art from from *res loquitur ipsa, quae semper valet plurimum* 'the thing itself speaks and that is always of the utmost value'. Cicero Pro Milone 53.

Sic utere tuo ut alienum non laedas 'use your own in such a way that you do not hurt (injure) another's'. Do not drive your car so as to smash up other people's vehicles and do not cause or permit evil smells to escape from your septic tank so as to asphyxiate and injure your neighbour. The expression is used by lawyers usually in relation to damage caused by the acts or omissions of adjoining or neighbouring landowners and is fundamental to the tort of nuisance.

Sine die 'without a day'. An expression much used in the courts still when a trial or matter is adjourned to a date for resumption, which is not fixed. With no appointed day it may sometimes mean indefinitely. Appearing in the Compact Oxford English Dictionary this may be regarded as co-opted and part of the English language.

Uberrimae fidei 'of the greatest or utmost good faith'. This is a phrase which ought to be known and heeded by all. In the case of some contracts, where the related relevant facts are in the sole possession of one party, the law requires that full and *bona fide* disclosure of them be made to the other: in default the contract may be set aside, be voidable. These are called contracts '*uberrimae fidei*'. One such contract, which concerns us all, is that of insurance. In the case of such contracts full and frank disclosure of all facts and matters which are asked, and/or which are not specifically asked but which the insured may reasonably be expected to think might affect the risk, should be made to the insurer at the outset and (if there be any material change of circumstance) at the time of any renewal. An insured fails to do so at his peril.

Ultra vires 'over or outside powers'. Beyond or in excess of powers conferred. Thus if a statute affords powers for the control of alcohol sales, these could not validly be used to control the sale of narcotics: any attempt to do so would be *ultra vires* and void. The notorious Lord Chief Justice Jeffreys at the bloody assizes of 1685, after the rout of the protestant Duke of Monmouth at the battle of Sedgemoor by forces of the Catholic King James II, presided over some travesties of trials in which scant regard was permitted to evidence which did not go to guilt. One was of Lady Alice Lisle, an elderly widow who, it was said, had harboured and fed two wretches fleeing from the battlefield. She was found guilty in a shameful charade of a trial and sentenced to be burned alive. Such a sentence was not within the judge's powers, was *ultra vires*, and was commuted to beheading. Note that at this time the judges held office *durante beneplacito:* see *quamdiu se bene gesserint* above.

SLAVERY

AD 2007 saw the 200th Anniversary of The Slave Trade Act 1807, passed after a prolonged and bitter struggle against powerful vested commercial interests. The anti-slavery society had been formed in 1787 by Thomas Clarkson, Granville Sharp and William Wilberforce (1759-1833). The son of a wealthy Hull merchant, Wilberforce had become MP for Hull in 1784 and developed a close friendship with William Pitt the younger, who, when Prime Minister promised to try to abolish the slave trade. Supported by Fox and Burke he kept his promise, but the Act of 1807 was not passed until after his death by his great rival Fox. The Act was insufficiently tightly drawn and not all embracing so that a further Anti Slave Trade Act 1843 was necessary 'for the effectual suppression of the slave trade'.

So obnoxious to civilised man is the idea of a person owning and exploiting another rightless human being, that a little of the slave-related law of Rome, that pinnacle once of world civilisation, is noteworthy and is below set out.

In Roman Law the slave was a chattel but endowed with reason. He was the object of rights but had none himself. In the early republic there were very few slaves, but over the years as the Roman Empire expanded by conquest and the principal way of falling into slavery was defeat in war, they became very numerous and meant big business. Unlike slavery in Britain's 18th century, which ravaged Africa and brought black men from the tribes (sometimes sold by their chieftains, sometimes captured by raiding parties) in terribly brutal and callous conditions to menial tasks in Britain (but mainly to sugar and other plantations in America), the Roman slave was on the whole white and was often well educated, capable of acting as private secretaries and of teaching medicine, oratory, mathematics etc. In particular those from Greece and the Near East.

Not until the end of the first and second centuries AD was any attempt made to regulate a master's treatment of his slave. The results were comparable with that afforded to animals by modern law. Early in the empire a master was forbidden to send his slave to fight with wild beasts in the arena without a magistrate's fiat, and under the emperors Hadrian and Antoninus Pius a master could be compelled to sell a slave who took refuge from intolerable cruelty at the foot of a statue of the emperor. Treatment varied enormously. Cato tells us that in agriculture it was more economical to work a slave to death and buy another one than properly to feed, clothe and accommodate him. The domestic slave's position was little better. It was customary for one's door-keeper to be chained to his post. Those educated were however generally respected and well treated, often virtually as free men. Many were actually freed.

The Royal Mint struck a £2 coin to commemorate AD 2007 as the bicentenary of the abolition of the slave trade. An edge inscription was not in Latin but was taken from a seal commissioned by Josiah Wedgwood and read 'Am I not a man and a brother'.

Calones. Name given to personal slaves taken with them on campaign by high ranking Roman soldiers. Comparable to the batman, the British army officer's personal attendant.

Et libertas quidem est, ex qua etiam liberi vocantur, naturalis facultas eius, quod cuique facere libet, nisi si quid aut vi aut iure prohibetur. 'and freedom from which the word freedom in its application to men is derived, is the natural capacity for each of us to do what we please unless prevented either by force or by the law'. Justinian Institutes Lib I. Tit III 1.

Et quidem summa divisio de iure personarum haec est, quod omnes homines aut liberi sunt aut servi 'the main distinction in the law of persons is this, that all men are either free or slaves. Gaius i.9. In Rome everyone was assigned a status by the law.

Ingenuus is est, qui statim, ut natus est liber est, sive . . .. 'A person is *ingenuus* who is free from the moment of his birth . . .' Various detailed criteria governed how one might be born free . . . Justinian Institutes Lib I. Tit. IV.

In pari delicto. See under Law and Justice at page 74 above.

In servorum condicione nulla differentia est. In liberis multis differentiae sunt: aut enim ingenui sunt aut libertini 'in the position of slaves there is no distinction. There are however many distinctions among free persons. They are either born free or have been set free.' Justinian Institutes Lib I. Tit III.5.

Libertini sunt, qui ex justa servitate manumissi sunt.

Manumissio autem est datio libertatis 'freedmen are those who have been manumitted from legal servitude. Manumission is the giving of freedom.' *Manumissio* was the word used for the freeing of a slave. Justinian Institutes Lib I. Tit III.4.

Non tamen cuicunque volenti manumittere licet. Nam is, qui in fraudem creditorum manumittit, nihil agit . . . ' However it is not every master who wishes may manumit, for manumission in fraud of creditors will be of no effect.' Gaius i.37. The number of slaves who could be manumitted (freed) on death by will was limited. If a Roman owned a lot of slaves, a dying gesture freeing them all would be permitted by law only up to a specified number.

Noxa autem est corpus, quod nocuit, id est servus: noxia ipsum maleficium, veluti furtum, damnum, rapina, iniuria '*Noxa* is the body which has done a wrong, that is the slave. *Noxia* is the wrong itself such as theft, damage, violent robbery or injury'. Justinian. Institutes. Book 4 Tit8.1.
Now go to *summa autem* below.

Pertinax. Name of a Roman emperor in the year AD 193. He tried to curb the excesses of the Praetorian Guard and generally moved too fast in attempting to effect change. He ruled for only 87 days before being brutally murdered by soldiers on the Palatine (one of the seven hills of Rome). His point of interest here is that he is an example of social mobility at the time. His father had been a slave. Slave to emperor in one generation.

Re(g)ina liberta coniunx 'Queen freedwoman (and) spouse'. In the museum of Arbeia in South Shields is to be seen an 1800 year old stone funerary monument to a young woman found outside the nearby Roman fort. She is sculpted not in an English or a Roman style and the ravages of time have worn away most of her face. From the above and from further inscriptions we learn however that she had come from a tribe inhabiting the St. Albans area (the *Catuvellauni* see page 110 below), became a slave, was freed, married one Barates and died aged 30. Barates was from Palmyra: a Syrian! Trading with the Romans, it is to be inferred, he had found, bought, freed and married his 'queen' but she had left him behind in life. Another inscription in his own language reveals to us his grief: 'Regina freedwoman of Barates, alas'. Sculpted in the best Palmyrene style, the monument is almost unique in Britain.

Servi autem aut nascantur aut fiunt. Nascuntur ex ancillis nostris: fiunt aut jure gentium, id est ex captivitate, aut jure civile, veluti cum homo liber major viginti annis ad pretium participandum sese venumdari passus est 'slaves are either born or become so. They are so born when their mother is a slave. They become so either by the law of nations, that is by captivity or by the civil law, as when a free person agrees to be sold on the basis that he should share in the price given for him'. Justinian Institutes Lib I. Tit III.4.

Servi autem ex eo appellati sunt, quod imperatores captivos vendere iubent ac per hoc servare nec occcidere solent: . . . 'slaves are described as *servi* because generals order them to be sold and thus preserve them and do not put them to death'. Justinian Institutes Lib I. Tit III.3. The usual way to become a slave in the first instance was to be captured in war and sold by victorious generals with this automatically acquired status. This was a consequence of defeat in war accepted in the known world.

Servitus 'slavery' hence servitude, though the Romans had another word for slavery, *servitudo*. Servitude means 'the state of being a slave' or in 2007 more often the state of being utterly subject to the power and imposed restriction of another.

Servitus autem est constitutio juris gentium, qua quis dominio alieno contra naturam subicitur. 'slavery is an institution of the law of nations whereby a man is made the property of another contrary to natural right'. Justinian Institutes Lib I. Tit III.2.

The institution of slavery was the one area where there appeared to be irreconcilability between the Roman concept of *ius gentium* (law of nations) and *ius naturale* (natural law) a difference between the *de facto* 'in fact' position and the 'ought to be' position.

Servus 'a slave'.

Sic volo, sic iubeo, sit pro ratione voluntas 'I wish thus, I order thus: let my will be the reason'. Juvenal vi.223. You will do as you are bid because I say so. Well known passage of Juvenal (AD 35 - c.130) who wrote of a dominant wife talking, not to her slave, but to her husband who, without giving reason, she demands should crucify a blameless slave. Crucifixion was not an unusual *in terrorem* Roman punishment. After the celebrated escaped gladiator Spartacus, who had organised and trained an army which inflicted several defeats on Roman legions, was ultimately overwhelmed and defeated in 71 BC, six thousand of his captured comrades were crucified on the Appian Way between Rome and Capua. The logistics of what must have been a very protracted operation are unimaginably awful. Possibly the most compelling example of Virgil's famous observation: *una salus* *nullam sperare salutem* 'the only safe course for the vanquished is to expect no mercy'. Aeneid ii 354. See under AD 2007 above.

Summa autem ratione permissum est noxae deditione defungi: namque erat iniquuum, nequitiam eorum ultra ipsorum corpora dominis damnosam esse 'it is with the greatest of (good) reason that the master should be allowed to settle any claim by surrender of the offender. For it would be inequitable that the master should suffer any loss beyond that of the slave himself.' Justinian. Institutes. Book 4.Tit 8.2. This entitlement is termed 'noxal surrender' and was not available to a master of whom it could be shown that he could have prevented the slave's wrongdoing. No such easy avoidance of obligation to pay the millions of pounds due where your servant or agent acting in the course of his employment negligently renders another permanently disabled or paraplegic exists today (though the primary responsibility is yours, indemnity will generally be contractually forthcoming from your insurer).

ECCLESIASTICAL
AND BIBLICAL

Several entries under this head (and a few elsewhere) are taken from the Vulgate. This is the name given to the Holy Bible as translated into Latin, from sources in Aramaic, Hebrew and Greek in the 4th century by St. Jerome, commissioned by Pope Damasus I. It was finally revised in 1592 by Pope Clement VIII, after a series of interruptions caused by the deaths, each after only a very short term in office, of no less than three Popes, which followed a much criticised and rejected revised version produced by Pope Sixtus V in May 1590. The Vulgate has been used in much of the western church since the seventh century. The version currently in use is the Clementine edition.

Advocatus diaboli 'devil's advocate'. See under Social at page 58 above.

Benedictus benedicat See under Social above at page 59 .

Dominus custodiat introitum tuum et exitum tuum. See under Holiday/Tourism above at page 30.

Dominus vobiscum 'The Lord be with you'.

Ecce homo 'behold the man'. Words used by Pontius Pilate as he showed Christ to the mob wearing a crown of thorns. Used as the title to a number of paintings depicting the scene.

Ego sum alpha and omega principium et finis dicit Dominus Deus 'I am alpha and omega saith the Lord God, the beginning and the ending'. Vulgate. Revelation 1.7.8. Alpha and omega are respectively the first and the last letters in the Greek alphabet. The word 'alphabet' is based on the first two letters of the Greek alphabet, alpha and beta.

Et dicit eis quid timidi estis modicae fidei 'and he said unto them, why are ye fearful, O ye of little faith.' Vulgate St. Matthew 8.26. Jesus spoke to his disciples. The last five words (of what is the King James authorised Holy Bible translation) constitute a much-used expression in the English language.

Extra omnes 'all (or everyone) out'. Words used to direct all officials to leave when the cardinals, having sworn an oath of secrecy, are about to assemble inside the conclave (a lockable room, from the Latin *clavis* a key) in the Vatican's Sistine Chapel to elect a new Pope: last heard on 18th April 2005 when, following the death of Pope John Paul II, one hundred and fifteen cardinals assembled and the next day their spokesman announced (with the traditional words *nuntio vobis gaudium magnum: habemus Papam* ' I announce to you a great joy: we have a Pope') election of the German Cardinal Joseph Ratzinger as Pope Benedict XVI. He is on record as having described the Mass in any language other than Latin as a 'tragic breach' and in his Sacramentum Caritatis 'sacrament of love' in March 2007 urged revival of the Gregorian Chant and wider use of Latin in the Mass.

Extra omnes are two Latin words which dogs, disposed to behave riotously in the house, ought to be trained to understand and act upon. It has been queried whether dogs have souls. Of course they have.

Life is full of surprises but it must be a remarkable surprise to wake up one morning and realise "My goodness! (not my God), I'm the Pope".

Fiat lux 'let there be light'. From Genesis 1:3 in the Vulgate. Motto of Berkeley University of California.

Fidei Defensor See *Dei Gratia* under Coinage.

Index librorum prohibitorum 'list of prohibited books'. A list of books which Roman Catholics are forbidden to read. The list has not been updated for some time and has fallen into disuse. In the 16th century the works of Erasmus were on the Spanish list of prohibited books. There was also an *index expurgatorius*, a list of books, expurgated versions of which the faithful were permitted to read.

Lapis angularis 'cornerstone'. The stone which the builders refused is become the head *stone* of the corner. Psalm 118; 22. Woven delightfully into Somerset Maugham's novel 'Catalina' set in very Catholic 16th century Spain.

Non Angli sed angeli 'not Angles but angels.' Observation attributed to Pope Gregory 1st (before he became Pope) when he saw fair haired Anglo-Saxon youths for sale in Rome's slave markets.

He was Pope from AD 590–604.

Nulli malum pro malo reddentes 'render unto no man evil for evil'. See under Social above at page 14. Integral part of that multi-sourced prayer:

> 'Go forth into the world in peace
> Be of good courage,
> Hold fast to that which is good;
> Render unto no man evil for evil;
> Support the weak;
> Help the afflicted;
> Honour all men.'

With the addition perhaps of 'be of good cheer', what better code of living for humans could there be?

Nunc dimittis 'now you dismiss'. From St. Luke's gospel 2:v:29 *nunc dimitttis servum tuum, Domine* 'loosely rendered as 'Lord now lettest thou thy servant depart in peace according to thy word'. Said or sung in the Anglican Church in accordance with the provisions of the book of Common Prayer. The *nunc dimittis* is also known as 'The Song of Simeon'.

Quia pulvis es et in pulvem reverteris 'for dust thou art and unto dust thou shalt return'. Vulgate. Book of Genesis 3:19. To be remembered by those who get above themselves.
We are endlessly reminded;. *Pulvis et umbra sumus* 'we are dust and shadow'. Horace Odes IV.vii.16. 'Earth to earth, ashes to ashes, dust to dust.' Part of the Order for the Burial of the Dead in the Church of England Book of Common Prayer.

Quod scripsi scripsi 'what I have written I have written'. St. John xix.22 in the Vulgate. Above Christ on the cross Pontius Pilate caused to be placed an inscription in Hebrew, Greek and

Latin, which in the Latin read *I(J)esus Nazarenus Rex I(J)udae-orum.* 'Jesus of Nazareth King of the Jews.' Frequently abbreviated to *INRI* on crucifixes to be seen in churches (particularly Roman Catholic). because there was no letter J in the Latin language. The Jews and the chief priests took exception to this assertion and protested, denying vigorously its truth. Pilate was unmoved and answered with the words *quod scripsi scripsi.*

Sic transit Gloria mundi 'thus passes away the glory of the world.' Words spoken at the investiture of a new Pope when white flax is burned signifying the transitory nature of worldly glory.

King Philip II of Spain (1527 – 98) died in wretched conditions of sickness and associated squalor, and was moved to comment upon that to which the most powerful man in the world had come.

Tantum religio potuit suadere malorum 'religion was able to persuade to so great a mass of evils'. Lucretius *De rerum natura* 'on the nature of things' .i.107. He lived c. 99-55 BC. He had human sacrifice in mind. Subsequent history has seen this general observation borne out in abundance in Europe. The burnings of heretic Cathars through the Dominican Inquisition in 13th century France; in the 16th century in Spain by the Spanish Inquisition at the instance of the notorious Tomas de Torquemada's Holy Office and in England at the instance of Mary Tudor, recorded in all their awfulness by Foxe's *Book of Martyrs,* at Smithfield and in Oxford, where there stands a memorial to Archbishop Cranmer and Bishops Latimer and Ridley. And that famous utterance of Latimer as the flames rose from the faggots. "Be of good comfort Master Ridley. We shall this day light such a candle, by God's grace' in England as I trust shall never be put out". More recently the vicious troubles in Northern Ireland and in 2007 as Shia Moslems murder and maim Sunnis and vice versa in Iraq. Blaise Pascal (1623-62) .added his thought on the subject: 'men never do evil so completely and cheerfully as when they do it in the name of religious conviction'. Pensées.

Tu ne quaesieris, scire nefas, quem mihi, quem tibi finem di dederint. 'do not try to discover, for we are not allowed to know what end the gods will have ordained for me or for you. Horace Odes I.xi.i. Mankind tries but knows no more today.

Urbi et orbi 'to the city and to the world.' Pope Benedict XVI made his first speech on 20th April 2005. It was *urbi et orbi*. The city is Rome.

Vade in pace 'go in peace'.

COINAGE

Roman coins, some minted, used and found in what was the Roman Province of Britannia, are inscribed with many and varied inscriptions, naturally in Latin. A few are identified and considered below. When looking at their inscriptions remember that the letter V is the equivalent of the English U. Coinage struck in England after the Roman occupation has borne Latin inscriptions since Viking and Anglo-Saxon times. These are usually biblical, alluding generally to protection of the King/ Queen, the Kingdom or of the integrity of the coin itself. Some of these are considered below. *Tueatur Unita Deus* appears inscribed on the 2007 £5 Crown Piece is the most recent and is very interesting. See below and under AD 2007 at page 24 above.

Decus et tutamen. See *Has nisi* below.

Dei gratia 'by the grace of God'. Current British coinage bears the inscription 'Elizabeth II D.G. REG. F.D. which stands for: *Elizabeth II Dei Gratia Regina Fidei Defensor* 'Elizabeth the second by the grace of God, Queen, Defender of the Faith'. *Fidei defensor* , 'Defender of the Faith' is a title bestowed upon King Henry VIII by Pope Leo X in 1521 in recognition of Henry's book defending the seven sacraments against Martin Luther. Henry retained the title in relation to the breakaway Anglican Church, of which he made himself head, after he ceased to be a Roman Catholic. It is a title held by the British Monarch ever since as head of the Church of England. In September of 2007 Prince Charles let it be known that he prefers 'Defender of Faith'.

Dirige Deus gressus meos 'Lord direct my steps'. Inscription on a five pound piece of Queen Victoria.

Dum spiro spero 'while I breathe (live) I hope'. Inscription on coins (stamped on square pieces of silver sheet melted down from plate) of King Charles I minted at Pontefract following his capture by the Parliamentarians. After the King's execution in 1648/9 (numismatic publications point to the dual date as above. The King was executed in February and there was at the time disagreement as to exactly when the year began) the inscription was changed to *post mortem patris pro filio* 'for the son after the death of the father'. Used also during the siege of Pontefract was the inscription *hanc Deus dedit* 'God has given us this' (that is the crown).

Fidei Defensor See Dei Gratia.

Fel Temp Reparatio. Inscription on a coin of the emperor Constantius II. It appears to be an abbreviation of *Felix (felicium?) Temporum Reparatio* 'happy times renewed (restored)' nicely otherwise translated as 'happy days are here again.' In AD 337 the emperor Constantine died leaving three sons separately to rule over three parts of his ungovernably vast empire [Constantine II, Constantius II and Constans]. The coin is of circa AD 348, and such then was the terrible turmoil in the empire that it is difficult to understand how such an inscription could have been justified. Probably it was wishful thinking public relations. It is an inscription (in abstracto, the political climate was very different) which doubtless Gordon Brown would like to adopt in his new office. *Sed quaere*, would it be justified in the banking chaos of September 2007 or be probably on the same basis?

Has nisi periturus mihi adimat nemo 'on pain of death let no one remove these [letters] from me'. Words cut into the rim of crowns and half crowns of Oliver Cromwell c. 1656. A warning to those who might be tempted to debase the coinage by filing or scraping from the edges and collecting the valuable metal. To prevent this practice, known as 'clipping', all early large milled silver coinage had cut into the edge the inscription *decus et tutamen*. Today some one pound coins of England and Northern Ireland bear the same inscription likewise cut into their rims: translated as 'an ornament and a safeguard.' Since these coins are now struck in base metal of little value, the 'safe-guard' is against forgery, which is thus made much more difficult. The Scottish and Welsh coins have their own inscriptions on the rim. *Nemo me impune lacesssit* and *pleidiol wyf I'm Gwlad* (Welsh) respectively: 'no one attacks me with impunity' and 'true am I to my country' from the Welsh National Anthem. The words *decus et tutamen* are from Virgil's Aeneid V, 262. and are descriptive of an exquisitely crafted piece of armour as 'an ornament and a protection'.

Ides. In the Roman calendar the *Ides* fell on what is now 15th March, May, July, October and on 13th of all other months. The *Ides* features in Shakespeare's Julius Caesar.

Caesar 'I hear a voice shriller than all the music, Cry Caesar.'
  'Speak; Caesar is turned to hear'.
Soothsayer 'Beware the *Ides* of March'.

After Caesar had been murdered on the *Ides* of March a coin inscribed with *Brut Imp.*, 'Brutus Commander' and bearing the head of Marcus Brutus was struck in 43 or 44 BC by the army headed by Caesar's assassins. On the reverse is depicted a *pileus* (a hat-like object worn by freed [manumitted] slaves and a symbol of freedom) between two daggers above the inscription ID-MAR (sometimes EID-MAR) symbolising liberty restored by the death of the tyrant Caesar. All that is missing is blood dripping from the daggers. Given the power struggle and civil wars between Romans that ensued, a *pileus* was scarcely an appropriate symbol. The reverse of this coin is illustrated below beneath the heading 'Historical' on page 98.

Imp. C Domitianus P.F Avg. imp. See under Roman Emperors at page 126 below.

Inimicos eius induam confusione 'as for his enemies I shall clothe them with disorder'. Psalm 132,18. Inscription on shillings of Edward VI struck at Durham House, Strand. King Edward VI was only nine years old when he ascended the throne in1547. He died from consumption after only six years as king. Others ran for him a country in religious turmoil, suffering rampant inflation and going to war with Scotland, which allied with France. Enemies of the very young beleaguered King perhaps needed to be clothed in disorder. The words which immediately follow those above set out in Psalm 132 are: (translated) 'but upon himself shall his crown flourish'.

Pax missa per orbem 'peace sent through the world'. Inscription on a farthing of Queen Anne.

Tueatur unita Deus 'may God guard those united'. See under AD 2007 above at page 24. On his coinage King James 1st of England, 6th of Scotland used a number of other inscriptions related to unity of the Kingdoms: *faciam eos in gentem unam* 'I shall make them one nation'. Ezekiel, 37, 22. *Quae Deus conjunxit nemo separet* 'what God has joined together let no man put asunder.' St. Matthew 19.6. (do the Scottish Nationalists in their pursuit of independence defy God's will?). These words are to be seen in the form for solemnisation of matrimony in the Church of England Book of Common Prayer. *Henricus Rosas Regna Jacobus* 'Henry united the roses James united the Kingdoms' (a reference to the wars of the roses [the red rose of Lancaster and the white rose of York] which came to an end with the defeat of the Yorkists at Bosworth Field and the accession in 1485 of King Henry VII who married Elizabeth of York). And finally an inscription chosen by the King himself from Psalm 68,1: *Exurgat Deus et dissipentur inimici eius* 'let God rise up and his enemies be scattered'.

Vigebit in omne aevum 'he shall thrive throughout his latter years (in old age). Inscription on the reverse of the 'pattern' penny of King George III dated 1799. He reigned thereafter until his death in 1820 aged 81. The latter part of his 59 year reign saw England through the Napoleonic wars championed by such luminaries as William Pitt (the younger; Chancellor of the exchequer at the age of 23 and Prime Minister at 24), the Duke of Wellington and Lord Nelson.

Vivat Regina 'may The Queen live' usually translated as 'long live the Queen'. The words have been recently inscribed around and above a fanfare of three Royal Trumpets on the reverse of a 2006 £5 silver crown struck by The Royal Mint for the 80th birthday of HM Queen Elizabeth II. The coin is legal tender (but at a premium! Acquisition initially costs more than £5). The words (*vivat Rex* 'long live The King') were incorporated in Sir Hubert Parry's anthem 'I was glad'; processional music written for the coronation of King Edward VII and sung at all coronations since. If this music is performed the words (*vivat rex* or *regina* as appropriate) should be included only if the performance is in Westminster Abbey and they are shouted by the scholars of Westminster School.

The expression should be compared with *Rex* or *Regina nunquam moritur* 'the King/Queen never dies'. A legal expression referring to the theory of a continuing monarchy. 'The King is dead, long live the King!' After all, since all criminal prosecutions are brought at the suit of the Monarch (*Rex* or *Regina versus* . . . or R v . .) they cannot, when a King or Queen dies, cease or be held in abeyance pending the coronation of a successor

HISTORICAL

It is scarcely possible to peruse Latin words and phrases without touching upon history which invites explanatory narrative. Below are set out some random and possibly eccentric examples which speak for themselves. Emphasis is on Britannia and her early inhabitants and a map showing approximately the lands which they occupied follows at page 110 below.

Albinus. Clodius Albinus the Roman governor of Britannia in AD193, who was proclaimed emperor of Rome by the legions under his command after the brutal murder of the essentially decent emperor Pertinax by the Praetorian Guard. Coinage was minted so depicting him. One senator of considerable wealth, however, Didius Julianus, bought the emperorship at auction! But there remained three other claimants, one of whom was Septimius Severus. He quickly disposed of and executed Julianus. Then, by a combination of careful planning and deception, he defeated in battle both other claimants and became undisputed emperor. He disposed of Albinus and his wife and children with a terrible show of *in terrorem* brutality.

Afflavit Deus et dissipantur 'God blew and they are scattered'. Reference to the storms which went a long way to defeat the Spanish Armada sent by King Philip II of Spain in his attempted conquest of England in 1588.

Boadicea (real name *Boudicca*). A monument to her memory, as a symbol of freedom and the need to fight tyranny and injustice whatever the odds or the cost, is to be seen on the Thames Embankment close to Big Ben where she stands looking resolute and determined in her chariot. Prasutagus, king of the *Iceni* had managed peaceful co-existence with the occupying Romans. On his death in AD 64 however his lands were taken over and plundered: his Queen, Boudicca, was flogged and his daughters raped; all with the connivance of the Roman procurator, Decianus Catus. Boudicca's reaction was swift. Joined by the *Trinovantes* she led an uprising . Colchester (*Camulodunum*), St. Albans, (*Verulamium*) and London (*Londinium*) were sacked without quarter given and the Roman 9th legion was virtually annihilated. The Roman governor, Suetonius Paulinus, had however been campaigning in Anglesey. He immediately came south with a large and experienced force. Boudicca made rousing addresses to her followers as she drove in her chariot around the tribes with her daughters (recorded in Tacitus. Annals of Imperial Rome). But the rebels were crushed. Knowing what to expect for herself Boudicca committed suicide. Roman vengeance was terrible as survivors were mercilessly hunted down. See Classicianus under Holiday/Tourism above at page 27 above. See too page 110.

Britannia. The name given to Britain when she became a Roman Province in AD43. A personalised Britannia first appeared on the reverse of coins struck by the Emperor Hadrian. AD 117-

138. She has appeared on numerous English coins minted initially during the reign of Charles II and thereafter. See Hadrianus under Holiday and Tourism at page 30 above.

Caractacus. Name (correct name *Caratacus)* of a British chieftain who resisted the emperor Claudius' invasion of Britain in AD43. He was defeated and captured but escaped and rallied other tribes to stout defence of their lands until finally defeated in AD51, when he fled, ready to fight again, only to be handed over to the Romans by the queen of the *Brigantes*. Together with his family he was taken to Rome in chains to face death, the fate ordinarily meted out to leaders vanquished by the Romans. Lesser beings were usually sold into slavery. In Rome however word of his brave exploits had earned for him a certain curious admiration. Paraded before the people in manacles he approached the emperor Claudius's dais and addressed him (presumably in Latin) with such a forthright dignity and eloquence (recorded in Tacitus Book 12.32) that the emperor was moved and responded with clemency, releasing him and his family. A rare exception to Virgil's *una salus victis nullam sperare salutem.* 'the only safe course for the vanquished is to expect no mercy.Aeneid ii 354.

Cassivellaunus. Name of the king of the largest and most formidable of the southern British tribes, the *Catuvellauni*, which resisted Julius Caesar's second landing in Britain in 54 BC. He was forced to seek terms. See page 110 below.

Carausius. See Classis Britannica under military/naval at page 106 below.

Civis Romanus sum 'I am a Roman (citizen)'. Towards the

end of the Republc it was not lawful for a Roman citizen to be bound or beaten and such a plea had to be investigated. The expression appears as used by Cicero as prosecutor (In Verrem II.v.162), where he dwells upon the flagrant transgression of this right by Verres, the brutal and corrupt governor of Sicily. The verdict of guilty was a great triumph and not expected, given bribery, the accused's powerful allies and a defence conducted by the celebrated lawyer, Q.Hortensius. See *nihil tam munitum* under AD 2000 above.

Better known perhaps is the story of St. Paul, to be found in Acts of the Apostles xxii. 25-29. When detained to be examined by scourging, he pointed out that he was born a Roman (citizen). This caused some consternation and 'the chief captain also was afraid, after he knew that he was a Roman (citizen), because he had bound him'. See too *Carino Civi. Rom* under Epitaphs at page 49 above.

Durotriges. Roman/Latin name of a tribe of Britons inhabiting what is now the Dorset area of England. This tribe occupied the famous Iron Age hill fort known as Maiden Castle near what is now Dorchester. See page 110 below. On a plateau above the surrounding countryside it affords uninterrupted views in all directions, making surprise attack impossible. Covering a very substantial area and completely surrounded by a double ditch (*fossa*), one very deep and steep and both at the top of an already steep incline (the whole to be seen to this day and well worth a visit) it must have seemed impregnable. The Romans arrived in Dorset in 43AD and shortly after Vespasian stormed the eastern entrance to the castle. The defenders, despite their positional advantage, seem to have been no match for the disciplined and well equipped Roman military machine. Probably they were swept away in a hail of Roman ballista bolts. Sir Mortimer Wheeler's archaeological excavations in the 1930s revealed the famous spinal vertebrae of a Durotrigian with the iron head of a Roman bolt lodged between them.

Nescire quid antequam natus sis acciderit, id est semper esse puerum 'not to know what happened before you were born, that is to be a child always'. Cicero. To know some history is of the greatest value: it alerts a man to the real world and to where he may stand in it, for the same awful wars and conflicts go on happening. We learn from experience that man learns very little from experience.

Satis diu vel naturae vixi vel gloriae 'I have lived long enough for the demands of nature or of fame'. Famous statement made by a world weary Cicero when he was aged 55 (in 51 BC). No philandering or ambition after 55? Most people didn't live so long then; even the three score years and ten of Psalm 90.10 is an under estimate today (the full text is worth noting: 'the days of our years are three-score years and ten: and if by reason of strength they be four-score years, yet is their strength labour and sorrow; for it is soon cut off and we fly away'. Reference perhaps to prospects for life with the State pension! At what age in 2007 might we reasonably feel disposed to quote these words of Cicero? They were spoken in a speech (*pro Marcello*) made to Caesar thanking him for pardoning M. Marcellus when the latter, as consul, had launched an attack on Caesar, which had set off civil war.

Scottorum malleus 'hammer of the Scots'. See under Holiday/Tourism at page 31 above.

Vare, redde legiones 'Varus, give me back my legions'. Suetonius Augustus 23. Publius Quinctilius Varus was commander of a large Roman force engaged in subjugating parts of Germany. In AD 9 he was persuaded by one Arminius to deviate from an intended route and to take his army through some dense parts of the Teutoberg Forest. There he was ambushed and his whole army (well in excess of three legions, more than 15,000 men) annihilated. Varus committed suicide. The ageing Emperor Augustus was greatly distressed by this disaster. He kept the anniversary as a day of mourning and inter-mittently throughout the remainng five years of his life would cry out in anguish with the above words.

Vercingetorix. Name of a Gallic hero who rallied and united most of the Gallic tribes to resist Julius Caesar's conquest of Gaul. Described by Caesar as 'a man of boundless energy', he emerged in 52 BC and ran a strategy of avoiding engagement with a Roman army. He attacked foraging parties and supply trains and cut off supplies of food by a scorched earth policy. Anxious not to be cornered, he avoided where possible defence of hill towns/forts. Success at Gergovia (that of his own tribe the *Arverni*) gave him the confidence to move into Alesia, some 30 miles north-west of modern Dijon. It was large and defensively well sited with steep slopes and rivers on two sides.

Apparently hemmed in, he arranged the gathering of a reliev-ing army intending that the Romans should be attacked front and rear by himself and by his allies when they arrived. In a remarkably short space of time Caesar caused to be built an elab-orate system of defences against frontal and/or rear attack: It consisted *inter alia* of ramparts, ditches (some water-filled), sharpened stakes set at a defensive angle in the ground and covered pits containing impaling spikes. A very large relieving

Gallic force duly arrived and, as planned, the Romans were attacked to front and to their rear in prolonged and bitter fighting and, though sorely tested, the Roman defences held and finally the Gauls were forced to retreat. To preserve his followers Vercingetorix, in a brave and most magnanimous way, surrendered himself up to Caesar. He was taken to Rome to be humiliated in Caesar's Gallic triumph and later to be put to death by strangulation in the *Tullianum*, that natural cave like execution dungeon at the foot of the Capitoline Hill in which so many met their end. The tourist can visit it today. Too true this time Virgil's *una salus victis nullam sperare salutem* 'the only safe course for the vanquished is to expect no mercy'.

MILITARY AND NAVAL

Pax Romana 'Roman peace' is an expression crediting the Romans with maintaining peace and stability in the known world. A look at the facts suggests that this may be only relative for Imperial Rome was almost permanently at war with someone or at least fighting to protect threatened borders of Empire. By the year AD383 Europe was threatened by barbarians and thereafter Roman troops were progressively withdrawn from Empire, including the Province of Britannia. Soon after AD 400 Hadrian's Wall ceased to be effectively manned, and by AD 410 Roman administration was virtually non-existent: The dark ages had begun. In this same year Rome was sacked by Alaric the Goth.

Aquila. Name given to the standard of a Roman legion. *Signum* was another word for the standard used by the legion's sub units and appears in the bubble dialogue of 'Le fils d'Asterix (one of the famous 'Asterix the Gaul' pictorial series). Good for the egos of young [all?] Frenchmen as Romans are depicted as being outwitted, humiliated and defeated by Gauls (Frenchmen). The fictitious Asterix is probably based on those chieftains whose names

ended with an x of which there are several mentioned in Caesar's
commentarii (notebook records of his conquest of Gaul: *De Bello
Gallico* 'About the Gallic War.'). The most famous of these was
Vercingetorix, king of the *Arverni*, forced eventually to surrender
in 46 BC after defeat by Julius Caesar's brilliance and bravery after
a long and heroic struggle. His magnificent dignity in defeat is
recorded at 7.89 of the *commentariii* and is to be contrasted with
Caesar's callously brutal treatment of him. An admirer recently
sought to acquire a coin depicting this French paragon. "You will
never get one" said the assistant of famous coin dealers. "Is that
because so few have been found?" inquired the would be
purchaser. "No, there are quite a lot, but every Frenchman wants
one! Every Frenchman who read of Asterix in his youth? See too
Vercingetorix under Historical at page 103 above.

Classis Britannica 'British fleet.' A Roman fleet was maintained in the province of Britannia to keep the English Channel
open as a commercial and military waterway. It operated from
Richborough (*Rutupiae*), Dover (*Portus Dubris*) and *Portus
Lemanis* at Stuttfall, Lympne, all in Kent. The fleet became of
particular importance in the third century A.D. when raids by
pillaging Saxon pirates became a serious menace. The founda-
tions of the British Fleet are generally associated with King
Alfred the Great A.D. 871–901. However, there was a truly
British Fleet (*de facto* at least) well before that, since in AD286
one Carausius, commander of the Roman North Sea Fleet,
declared himself independent of Rome and emperor of Britannia
and some parts of northern Gaul, including Boulogne
(*Gesoriacum*). An attempt to unseat the usurper by the (joint)
emperor Maximian was beaten off by Carausius's 'British' fleet
in 289.

At this time *Portus Lemanis* seems to have assumed considerable importance. Tiles and an altar were found there by Charles Roach Smith (excavating in 1850) bearing the inscription CLBR (*Classis Britannica*) as were a substantial number of coins of Carausius and of Allectus, by whom the former was murdered in AD293. Shortly after, in AD296, the (joint) Emperor Constantius I came to Britain, out-manouevered, defeated and killed Allectus. Roman rule was restored.

A famous gold medallion (struck at Trier and found at Arras, a copy of which is to be seen in the British Museum) shows the 'relief of London by combined operations' and the Emperor (Caesar), Constantius I, entering London and being received by a grateful personalised 'LON' (*Londinium*. 'London'). An inscription describes the emperor as *redditor lucis aeternae* 'restorer of eternal light'.

The sea has receded and *Portus Lemanis* is now inland. Only a scattering of broken masonry is to be seen below the escarpment overlooking Romney Marsh and beside the Royal Military Canal, which itself was constructed as a defence against the Napoleonic threat.

Calones see under Slavery at page 81 above.

Fustuarium. Name given to a Roman military punishment which involved beating to death with a rod any soldier who had shown cowardice and had thereby endangered others. For cowardice on a greater scale by a body of men there was *decimatio*, which meant the drawing of lots and the beating to death, again with rods, of one in ten. Certainly these were *in terrorem* measures, which ensured the most rigid of discipline in the Roman legions. Nothing to lose but your life!

Gladius hispaniensis 'Spanish sword'. A balanced cut and thrust short sturdy sword with a tempered steel blade carried by the Roman legionary. It was about 64-69 cm (2ft 6ins.) long with a blade some 5cm (2ins.) wide. A fearsome weapon in skilled hands used mainly as a stabbing instrument. Livy tells us how, in the First Macedonian war (197 BC), after the Greek's defeat, the soldiers of Philip V were horrified when they first saw men killed by this weapon. The carriers of long spears forming a phalanx were no match for legionaries armed with such a sword, once they managed to get to close quarters.

Quis fuit horrendos primus qui protulit enses? 'who was it who first invented terrible swords?' Tibullus. Roman poet c.54-19 BC. He was commissioned by the emperor Augustus in 30BC to deal wth a revolt in Aquitania. He served with distinction but never took to soldiering: something reflected in the above quotation. See *Gladius hispaniensis*.

Scutum 'a shield'. *Aqua scutum* 'water shield'. *Aquascutum* is the name given to John Emary's shop after he had developed a rain repellent cloth from which raincoats were made. The shop, which had opened in London's Regent Street in 1851, is now world famous, trading with the clothing brand concept 'Modern British Classics' and with the motto in its coat of arms, *in hoc scuto fidemus* 'in this shield we trust'.

Testudo 'tortoise or shell of a tortoise'. The word was used to describe a military formation used by Roman armies whereby legionaries advanced tightly packed together, those to the fore holding their large rectangular shields in front of them, those on the right and left flanks holding them respectively to their right and left sides, while those in the centre held them flat and tight together over their heads forming a roof. The whole body of men was thus 'encased' by shields and protected from arrows, sling-stones, spears and other missiles as they advanced to close quarters so as to be in a position to use the deadly short *gladius hispaniensis* see above.

Veni, vidi, vici 'I came, I saw, I conquered'. Famous words attributed to Julius Caesar (in Parallel Lives) by Plutarch. Often wrongly thought to have been related to Caesar's conquests in Britain in 55 and 54 BC, these words were said when he reported his victory at Zela over Pharnaces, King of Pontus in 47 BC. According to Suetonius the words were also used in Caesar's Pontic Triumph.

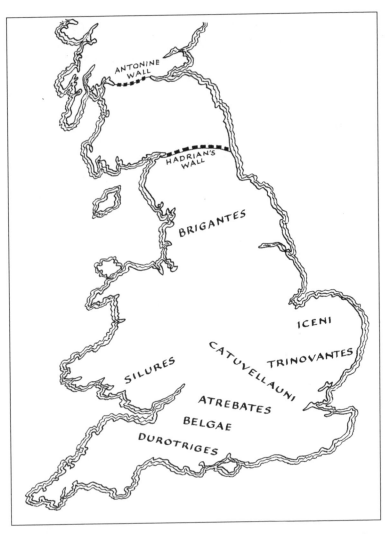

Map of England and Wales showing the location of Hadrian's Wall and of the Antonine Wall with the approximate areas occupied by the tribes of Britons in Roman times mentioned in the text.

THE BAYEUX TAPESTRY

AD 1066 is probably the best known date in English history; the
year of the Norman conquest of England by William, Duke of
Normandy (William the Conqueror, Guillaume le Conquérant)
and of the Battle of Hastings in which the English King, Harold
Godwinson, was defeated and killed. Notwithstanding, one good
reason for inclusion of the material following is that apparently
too many nowadays think that Gandalf won the Battle of
Hastings.

The events leading up to the battle, and the battle itself, are
recorded on a strip of linen (of which most, some 70 metres [or
230 feet] remains) embroidered pictorially with frieze and
accompanying explanatory commentary in Latin, thought to
have been produced in the decade following the battle by whom,
or at the instance of whom, is unknown. This tapestry is
displayed in Bayeux today where it can be seen. Harold's defeat,
and the consequent subjugation of the Saxon nation, is the only
time since the invading Romans in AD 43 established the
Province of Britannia (Julius Caesar's earlier landings in 55 and
54 BC having been little more than forays, successful against

some tribes in the south-east but which did not leave behind an administration) that this island has been invaded, despite alarming periods of threat posed by the Spanish Armada, Napoleon Buonaparte and Adolf Hitler. Set out below is a selection of extracts from the Latin commentary recording some of the main events seen on the tapestry. They are not in alphabetical order but follow the sequence of events.

Hic dederunt Haroldo corona Regis. Hic residet Harold rex anglorum 'here they gave the Royal Crown to Harold. Here enthroned is Harold King of England.' King Harold is to be seen sitting on a delightfully mediaeval throne holding an orb and a sceptre.

Hic Willelm dux iussit naves edificare 'here Duke William ordered the building of ships'. *Aedificare* might have been earlier and better Latin. The tapestry depicts Duke William in council followed by men busy building ships.

Hic trahunt naves ad mare: isti portant armas ad naves. et hic trahunt carrum cum vino et armis 'Here they drag ships to the sea These men carry weapons down to the ships. And here they pull a cart filled with wine and weapons'. A progression of men is depicted carrying spears, chain mail, swords and axes. A noticeably large barrel of wine is prominent in a man-pulled cart, obviously essential to a Frenchman going to war. *Arma* rather than *armas* would have been correct Latin.

Hic Willelm dux in magno navigio mare transivit et venit ad Pevensae 'here Duke William crosses in a big ship and comes to Pevensey'. Soldiers with shields in single sail Viking style open boats with carved heads to fore are depicted. In others are to be seen attended and unattended horses. It is unclear where is Duke Willliam himself. It has been estimated that some 400-450 ships ferried some 7000-8000 men and 2000 horses to England.

Hic exeunt caballi de navibus 'here the horses get out of the ships'. Two ships are to be seen behind those carrying out this operation. Someone in one appears to be having a good slug of the wine.

Et hic milites festinaverunt Hestingham ut cibum raper-entur ' and here the soldiers hurried to Hastings to secure food'. Foraging party.

Hic fecerunt prandium. et hic episcopus cibum et potum benedicit. Odo episcopus . . . . . 'here they have a meal and here the Bishop blesses the food and the wine (with the words *benedictus benedicat*?) Bishop Odo. . . .' They are to be seen sitting down to a grand served meal and a servant holds for the grandees a bowl and a cloth, evidently for the washing of hands. Odo was William's half brother and Bishop of Bayeux.

Hic milites exierunt de Hestenga et venerunt ad prelium contra Haroldum rege 'here the soldiers left Hastings and went to battle against King Harold'. The armoured horsemen are depicted setting out en masse. *Proelium* is the usual word for battle and *regem* would be correct grammar.

Hic Willelm dux alloquitur suis militibus ut preparent se viriliter et sapienter ad prelium contra Anglorum exercitu 'here Duke William exhorts his soldiers to prepare themselves like men and sensibly for the fight against the

English army.' *Prelium* appears again instead of *proelium* and *exercitu* should read exercitu<u>m</u>. Norman cavalry clash with English infantry, arrows and spears fly and axes and swords are swung in the immediately ensuing parts of the tapestry and suddenly the lower frieze, hitherto part decorated with heraldic beasts and birds, is strewn with dead bodies often lying pierced variously with arrows, swords and spears.

Hic ceciderunt simul Angli et Franci in prelio 'here both the English and the French fell simultaneously in the battle.' The battle clash grows fiercer as horses are up-ended and the lower frieze is littered with dead men and horses, abandoned weapons and one decapitated soldier. *Prelio* appears instead of *proelio*.

Et ceciderant qui erant cum Haroldo. 'here fell those who were with Harold. Suddenly the lower decorative border is filled with archers, arrows in their bows at the ready.and the main tapestry shows those about Harold being set upon and slain, their shields noticeably studded with arrows.

Hic Harold rex interfectus est 'here King Harold is killed.' Harold is depicted holding an arrow which has apparently entered through his right eye. The lower frieze is filled with men taking the valuable armour from slain soldiers and retrieving now ownerless swords.

Et fuga verterunt Angli 'and the English turned in flight'. So ended 14th October 1066 for the brave but luckless Harold Godwinson having had to do battle again some ten days following a gruelling march south after having defeated at Stamford Bridge the Norwegian King Harold Hardrada, aided by Tostig, the former's half brother, who had claimed his crown. The second battle, at Hastings, had been long and bloody. The central site was Senlac Hill: *sang lac* 'lake of blood'. The words *harold rex interfectus est,* as thy appear on the tapestry, are reproduced on the jacket of Winston S. Churchill's A History of the English–Speaking Peoples Volume 1, 'The birth of Britain', which tells, in fast moving succinct narrative, of the events which beset and overwhelmed the unfortunate Harold Godwinson. Throughout the later frames, where the lower frieze is strewn with lifeless slain bodies, the upper frieze continues to be filled with heraldic beasts and birds. Surely the words *et fuga verterunt angli* (in Latin or at all) have not since been used!

CLASSIFICATORY
(animals, fish, plants, reptiles etc)

Carolus Linnaeus (originally Carl von Linné) 1707-78, the Swedish naturalist and physician, was the first to use a binomial system for the naming and classifying of plants and animals. In Latin he gave each a generic name qualified by a specific adjective. His manuscripts and collections are kept at the Linnaean Society in London.

A selection of Latin classificatory names is set out below. The English names are not usually direct translations of the Latin. Only the English names in bold are in alphabetical order.

Bellis perennis. **Common Daisy**. Invasive of lawns and a joy or a disaster according as to how one feels about their presence.

Aesculus hippocastanum **Common Horse Chestnut**. Its large polished brown seeds are called 'conkers' and it is known to many as a 'conker' tree. Young children play a game called 'conkers' in which two adversaries' conkers have a hole bored through them and are suspended on knotted strings: one strikes the conker of the other alternately until one or other breaks. The number of conkers broken previously in successive contests by a losing (ultimately broken) conker is allocated to the most recent winning conker, as is the number which that winning conker may itself previously have gained. A competing conker will be known by the number which it has collected in this way. Thus one which has accumulated the equivalent of fifty six victories will be known as 'a fifty-sixer'. Much skill may be involved and many and varied treatments are used to harden competing conkers. To play conkers is thought by some to be dangerous unless safety equipment is worn.

Scomber scombrus. **Common Mackerel**. Beautifully designed for speed of travel through the water, this fish has lovely black on silver markings.

Talpa europaea. **Common Mole**. Has a most attractive thick black fur from which countrymen used to make moleskin waist-coats. Eats worms. Terribly destructive of lawns and impossible to drive away. Abundant. Certainly not an endangered species!

Quercus robur. **Common Oak**. The most usual of several species of English oak tree from which was built for hundreds of years the 'British Man of War', which served Sir Francis Drake and Lord Nelson.

Vipera berus **Common Viper or Adder**. Its potent venom is very dangerous. Recognisable by a black on yellow zigzag design along its body. Will usually retreat and will attack only if surprised or threatened.

Paravespula vulgaris. **Common Wasp**. Lives in colonies which expire in the autumn. Queen wasps survive and hibernate, amongst other places, in rooms in people's houses.

Amanita phalloides. **Death Cap**. The most poisonous European mushroom. Contains at least two deadly toxins. Superficially it can have an edible mushroom-like appearance. Take the greatest care.

Anobium pertinax. **Death Watch Beetle**. See General and Miscellanea at page 43 above

Papaver rhoeas. **Field Poppy**. Immortalised by James McRae's 1914-18 war poem 'In Flanders fields the poppies grow Between the crosses, row on row' and by the purchase each year of a poppy before Remembrance Sunday.

Natrix natrix **Grass Snake**. Too often these beautiful snakes are wantonly killed by those with snake phobia and unnecessarily by those who are ignorant that they are harmless or who cannot distinguish them from adders. Greenish brown in colour, it is readily recognisable by a yellow ring around its neck.

Apis mellifica. **Honeybee**. Both wild and encouraged into hives for the production of honey. Sting dangerous and may be lethal to those sensitive to it.

Picea abies. Known as **Norway Spruce**, this is the popular **Christmas Tree** of Central Europe and Britain.

Vanessa atalanta. **Red Admiral**. Common exotic red, black and white butterfly.

Coccinella septempunctata. **Seven-spot Ladybird**. Red with black spots, it is very common and its larvae eat aphids.,

Turdus philomelos. **Song Thrush**. An increasingly rare visitor to our gardens in the months April to October when it returns from its migration south.

Urtica dioica. **Stinging Nettle**. This common plant, was used by the Romans to brush aching and arthritic joints, especially backs. Tea, made from the leaves is supposed to have healing qualities.

Phallus impudicus. Translatied literally from the Latin this might be called 'lewd male member'. The form and appearance of this fungus is disconcertingly like the real thing. Known however as **Stinkhorn,** the mature fungus produces a disgusting smell.

Trifolium repens. **White Clover**. To find a four (as opposed to the usual three) leaf clover is supposed to bring good luck: they are very rare.

Sus scrofa. **Wild Boar**. Inhabits forests with undergrowth. Lives in herds. Widespread in Europe. Omnivorous and likes to eat grapes from vineyards in France. Once thought extinct in England, it is again becoming not uncommon in the forests and woodlands of the south.

Digitalis grandiflora. **Yellow Foxglove**. Extract from this plant is used medically to treat heart conditions.

ROMAN EMPERORS, TAKING THE PURPLE

Roman emperors wore purple, more particularly Tyrian purple, an ancient colour from a now obsolete dye. It was originally made by the Phoenicians (an ancient people from the eastern Mediterranean) in 1500 BC and became the colour of the robes of Kings. Pliny the elder told of the shellfish used in an elaborate manufacturing process, which made the dye very expensive. A great many Romans aspired to take the purple and become emperor but, given the fate of so many of those who actually did (see below), one has to wonder why and whether it was really a worthwhile risk.

Caesar. Gaius Julius Caesar was all but the first emperor of Imperial Rome. He was Dictator but almost certainly aspired to more before he was murdered in 44 BC by a group of senators, headed by Brutus and Cassius, who feared that his unrelenting quest for power would mean the end of the republic as, in the event it did anyway. Shakespeare's play, *Julius Caesar*, tells the history of this episode dramatically. For more about this remarkable ruthless genius, soldier, politician, writer and setter up of the Julian calendar, read Allan Massie's 'Caesar' and Christian Meir's 'Caesar'.

The best known of the Roman emperors (with the exception in the period AD 98-AD180 of those outstanding rulers of empire, Trajan, Hadrian, Antoninus Pius and Marcus Aurelius) are those eleven who followed Julius Caesar's death, their lives being written about in Suetonius' *De Vita Caesarum* (concerning the life of the Caesars). Suetonius, writing in the reign of Hadrian (117-138), was a secretary in the imperial palace and had access to the imperial archives: that is, until dismissed in 121/2 for some indiscretion concerning the emperor's wife. This work is available in Penguin Classics translated by Robert Graves called 'Suetonius The Twelve Caesars'. The first of these was Augustus (27BC-AD 14). The fate of those ten who followed him in taking the purple is astounding.

Augustus 27BC-AD14. The first emperor of Imperial Rome. A remarkable man. Aged nineteen at Caesar's death, he was thrust into political turmoil and civil war endangering his life, but he emerged triumphant to reign as emperor of Rome and most of the known world from 29BC until his death from old age in AD14. 'He found Rome built of brick. He left it built of marble'. Suetonius. Augustus 28. It is not possible in a book of this nature to do justice to the man and satisfactorily to say more. Read Allan Massie's novel 'Augustus' and Richard Holland's 'Augustus, Godfather of Europe'.

Tiberius AD 13-37. In his long reign he became disenchanted with the burdens of a ruler and retired to Capri, leaving administration effectively to one Sejanus who, in due course he came to suspect of plotting his overthrow. Skilfully he arranged the latter's death and advanced into old age. Becoming sick he came near to death but his sudden recovery so terrified his prospective successor, Caligula, who had advanced so perilously far in taking over, that he is thought to have arranged for the Prefect, Macro, to murder him by smothering. Read Alan Massie's 'Tiberius'.

Caligula Nickname. Real name Gaius Caesar Augustus Germanicus 37-41. The word 'caligula' meant 'little boot and was a name given to him by soldiers when, as a very young child, he wore little 'caliga', a hob-nailed boot worn by soldiers up to officer rank. Famous, rather notorious, as perpetrator of a large number of outrages and wanton cruelties. He survived several conspiracies, organised by those who felt unable to cope with more, before eventually being assassinated. Read Allan Massie's 'Caligula'.

Claudius 41-54. Invaded Britain in AD43 and founded thereby the Roman Province of Britannia. Murdered with poisoned mushrooms at the instance of Agrippina, his wife, in order to secure the succession of her son Nero. After Claudius' deification, the emperor Nero joked that mushrooms were the food of gods!

Nero 54-68. His reign began well but degenerated with persecution of the Christians, whom he blamed for the great fire in Rome, with his unsustainable extravagance, the murder of his mother and extravagant sexual excesses. He prided himself on his artistic talent and virtually his last words, as he managed an undignified suicide, were: *Qualis artifex pereo* ' what an artist I die'.

Galba 68-69. See *omnium consensu* under Political above at page 36. Murdered.

Otho 69. His reign lasted only three months. Civil war broke out as one Vitellius made claim to the purple. After suffering one defeat Otho, most impressively, committed suicide (and there were many at the time greatly moved by such a heroic and magnanimous end brought about by a bon viveur regarded by the senate with suspicion as a one time friend of Nero) to avoid further Roman bloodshed in a protracted civil war.

Vitellius 69. He remained emperor for only eight months. An unattractive character and no soldier, he was unable to contain an independent bid for power involving Vespasian. Defeated he sought to hide but was discovered and murdered by the soldiers.

Vespasian 69-79. He was present at the invasion of Britain by Claudius in AD43 and was still engaged in suppressing the Jewish revolt (which ended with the famous siege of Masada and the construction of an unimaginably massive ramp by Flavius Silva) when he was proclaimed emperor. He built the Colosseum (substantially, it was completed by his son, Titus) and is remembered for his famed remark when he proposed a tax on public urinals. Titus protested that such a tax was undignified. "*Pecunia non olet*" 'money doesn't smell' he replied. At the age of sixty nine (unusually old for those times) he fell ill and nearly collapsed but struggled to his feet then died maintaining that an emperor should die standing up.

Titus 79-81. In the year following his father's death he completed the Colosseum and followed this with one hundred days of games in which animals, gladiators and criminals were butchered in one way or another for entertainment and to court popularity with the people (*ad captandum vulgus* See under Political at page 34 above). It was during his short reign that

Vesuvius erupted and wiped out Pompeii. He is thought to have died from a fever but suspicion hangs over Domitian.

Domitian 81-96. Initially a good administrator. However he became progressively concerned for his own position and safety and ordered numerous executions until eventually his own personal attendants sought safety in his murder

End of theTwelve Caesars written about by Suetonius. Of these nine were murdered or committed suicide. Of the emperors who followed (before circa AD 286, when the empire split into western [Rome] and eastern [Byzantium later named Constantinople and now Istanbul] empires, ruled sometimes by one emperor but usually by two) a remarkably large percentage died violent deaths mainly by murder but also by suicide and a few in battle. Only some of those of greater interest are specifically mentioned here below.

Nerva 96-98. He accepted the role of emperor having been approached by the conspirators who had engineered Domitian's murder. In his16 month reign he was inadequate and unable to control the chaos which reigned and died in a fit of apoplexy.

Trajan 98–117 and Hadrian 117–138. See respectively under Holiday/Tourism above at page 27.

Antoninus Pius 138-161. In a long and peaceful reign he was strong, civilised and well liked. In England he built the turf Antonine Wall north of Hadrian's Wall (see page 110) and had a seated Britannia on the reverse of much of his coinage He acquired the word *pius* (meaning dutiful or respectful) as part of his name and died of illness.

Marcus Aurelius 161-180. He was joint emperor with his brother Lucius Verus who died in 169. Famed for his sensitive and revealing thoughts to be found in his written meditations.

Commodus 180-192 Son of Marcus Aurelius, he developed signs of megolomania and was eventually murdered by those fearful for their own lives. He is portrayed with great film-maker's licence in the film 'Gladiator'.

Pertinax 193, (murdered) **Didius Julianus 193** (murdered) and **Septimius Severus**. 193-211. See **Albinus** under Historical above at page 98.

Caracalla. Nickname of Aurelius Antoninus. (He was associated with and named after a hooded and lengthened Celtic garment known as a *caracullus*). Son of Septimius Severus, he was joint emperor from 211 with his brother Geta until he murdered the latter in the same year. In the following year he had put to death the eminent jurist Papinianus for refusing to justify in law that murder. He built the famous baths in Rome and was given to cruelty. Murdered in 217.

Between 217 and 286 there were some 25 further Roman Emperors of whom sixteen were murdered, three committed suicide, one was executed, three died in battle, one died from plague and **Carus** was struck by lightening in 283! Of these the emperor **Elagabalus** 218-212 warrants mention on account of his unbridled bi-sexual antics, which outraged the Rome of the times and the ancient writers. He was in the end murdred by the Praetorian Guard and his body thrown into the River Tiber.

Carausius Roman Emperor of Britain alone from 286 until

murdered in 293. See *Classis Britannica* under Military/Naval at page 106 above.

Valerian. 253-260. See *una salus victis . . .* above under AD 2007 at page 25.

Imp. C Domitianus PF Augustus. Abbreviation of: *'Imperator Caesar Domitianus pius felix Augustus.* 'Emperor Caesar Domitian dutiful happy Augustus'. Inscription on a Roman coin found near Oxford in 2004 and now in the Ashmolean Museum, Oxford. Note again that, when looking at inscriptions on Roman coins the present day letter U is represented by the symbol or letter V and sometimes I should be read as J, there being no J in the Latin alphabet. This emperor, previously virtually unknown to historians, appears to have been ruler of the breakaway Gallic (comprising Britain, part of Gaul and initially Spain) Empire sometime during the years 271-274. The grandeur of this kind of inscription accompanying the emperor's portrait in relief on coinage is possibly one reason why so many aspired to be emperor.

Constantine I 307-337. In the power struggle which followed his father's death, Constantine marched on Rome and against the usurper Maxentius. En route he saw a vision of the Cross of Christ in the heavens with the words *in hoc (signo) vinces* 'in this sign (the cross) you shall conquer'. He entered battle under Christian banners and was victorious when a pontoon bridge replacing the Milvian Bridge, which crossed the River Tiber, collapsed and drowned Maxentius. Constantine became emperor and a committed Christian, making christianity the official religion of the Empire. He did however pass a number of barbaric less than Christian Laws.

Valens 364-378 Credited by some with the beginning of the decline and fall of the Roman Empire. In the year 378 he decided to deal with the Gothic menace and personally led an army 60,000 strong against them at Adrianople, but was defeated, killed and never seen again.

Honorius 395-423 Emperor in the year 410, when the Romans finally left Britain. See introduction to Military/Naval at page 105 above.

Justinianus Justinian. Emperor 527-565. Christian, soldier, lawgiver, he was the last emperor to use Latin as the official language of imperial government. In 529 he made Christmas Day a public holiday.

For an informative and fascinating far more detailed work about the Roman Emperors, read 'Chronicle of the Roman Emperors' by Chris Scarre published by Thames and Hudson.

ROMAN NUMBERS

ANNO DOMINI MMVII

Arabic numerals	Roman numerals	Cardinals
1	I	unus
2	II	duo
3	III	tres
4	IV	quattuor
5	V	quinque
6	VI	sex
7	VII	septem
8	VIII	octo
9	IX	novem
10	X	decem
11	XI	undecim
12	XII	duodecim
13	XIII	tredecim
14	XIV	quattuordecim
15	XV	quindecim
16	XVI	sedecim
17	XVII	septendecim
18	XVIII	duodeviginti
19	XIX	undeviginti
20	XX	viginti

Arabic numerals	Roman numerals	Cardinals
21	XXI	unus et viginti
22	XXII	duo et viginti
28	XXVIII	duodetriginta
29	XXIX	unodetriginta
30	XXX	triginta
40	XL	quadraginta
50	L	quinquaginta
60	LX	sexaginta
70	LXX	septuaginta
80	LXXX	octoginta
90	XC	nonaginta
100	C	centum
101	CI	centum et unus
126	CXXVI	centum viginti sex
200	CC	ducenti
500	D	quingenti
600	DC	sescenti
1000	M	mille
2000	MM	duo mille

BIBLIOGRAPHY

In writing this book I have consulted many and varied sources.
Here are as many as I can remember using to a degree sufficient
to warrant mention.

A Dictionary of Latin Words and Phrases. James Morwood OUP 1998.
An Introduction to Roman Law. Barry Nicholas. Oxford. Clarendon
    Press 1961.
Asterix Gallus. Dargaud. Paris 1974.
Augustus. Allan Masssie. Sceptre 1988.
Biographical Dictionary. Chambers-Harrap Publishers Ltd. 2002.
    Edited by Una McGovern.
Britain in the Roman Empire. John Liversedge. Reader's Union.
    Routledge and Kegan Paul. London 1969.
Caesar. The Conquest of Gaul. Penguin Classics. Translated by S.A.
    Handford revised by Jane F. Gardiner. Penguin Books 1982.
Cases in Constitutional Law. D.L. Keir and F.H. Lawson. Oxford at
    the Clarendon Press 1954.
Chambers Twentieth Century Dictionary edited A.M. Mansfield OBE
    BA Oxon 1974.
Coins of England and the U.K. Spink and Son Ltd. Forty second
    edition 2007.
Chronicle of the Roman Emperors. Chris Scarre. Thames and Hudson
    1995.
Discover Dorset. The Romans. Bill Putnam. The Dovecote Press 2000.
Elements of Roman Law. R.W.Lee. Sweet and Maxwell 1956.
Epitaphs. Nigel Rees Bloomsbury 1993.
Goodbye Mr. Chips. James Hilton. Coronet Books. Hodder and
    Stoughton 1934.

Kennedy. The Revised Latin Primer. Seventh edition. Longman's Green and co 1898.

Kings and Queen's of England devised and edited by Eric R. Delderfield. David and Charles 1999.

Latin in Oxford. Compiled by Reginald H. Adams. Perpetua Press 1996.

Latin Quips at your fingertips. Rose Williams. Barnes and Noble Books 2001.

Lawyers' Latin. New edition 2006. John Gray. Robert Hale.

Long Live Latin. John Gray. Canis Press 2004.

Oxford in the history of the Nation. A.L. Rowse. Weidenfeld and Nicholson 1975.

Plants and Animals. Jan Tornan and Jivi Felix. Octopus Books 1975.

Reading Latin Epitaphs. A handbook for beginners. John Parker. Cressar Publications, Penzance.

Roman Castrum at Lymne. Facsimile edition of the report on the excavations of Charles Roach Smith, 1852. Published by Harry Margary, Lympne Castle, Kent.

Roman Law and Common Law. W.W. Buckland and Arnold D. Mc Nair 2nd edition revised by F.H. Lawson. Cambridge University Press 1952.

Roman Legionary 58 BC–AD 69. Ross Cowan. Osprey Publishing 2003.

Rome at War. Kate Gulliver, Adrian Goldsworthy and Michael Whitby. Osprey Publishing 2005.

Suetonius. The Twelve Caesars. Translated by Robert Graves. Penguin Classsics 1967.

Tacitus. The annals of Imperial Rome. Translated by Michael Grant. Penguin Classics 1989.

The Bayeux Tapestry by Mogens Rud. Christian Ejlers, Publishers Ltd. Copenhagan 1992.

The College Graces of Oxford and Cambridge. Compiled by Reginald Adams. Perpetua Press Oxford 1999.

The Compact Oxford English Dictionary. Second edition revised. Edited by Catherine Soanes OUP 2003.

The Concise Oxford Companion to Classical Literature. Margaret

Howatson and Ian Chilvers OUP 1996.

The Da Vinci Code and the Secrets of the Temple. Robin Griffith-Jones, Master of the Temple. Canterbury Press 2006.

The History and Conquests of Ancient Rome. Nigel Rodgers. Consultant Dr. Hazel Dodge FSA. Anness Publishing Ltd. 2004.

The Institutes of Gaius. Text and notes by F. de Zulueta. Oxford at the Clarendon Press 1958.

The Institutesof Justinian. Thomas Saunders M.A. Longmans Green and Co.1956.

The Oxford Dictionary of the Popes. J.N.D.Kelly. OUP 1988.

The Oxford Writer's Dictionary. Compiled by R.E.Allen. OUP 1981.

The Penguin Book of Historic Speeches. Edited by Brian MacArthur. Penguin Books 1996.

Wordsworth Dictionary of Bible Quotations. Martin H. Mansor. Wordsworth Reference 1995.

ENGLISH INDEX

Not comprehensive

ALPHABETICAL INDEX
OF LATIN ENTRIES

Exclusive of the heads Classificatory and Roman Emperors,
which are included in the English index